NEWLY REVISED AND TOPICAL

Every Boy's Handbook

HAMLYN

London • New York • Sydney • Toronto

First published 1960
Second impression 1962
First revised edition 1963
Second revised edition 1966
Third revised edition 1968
Fourth revised edition 1970
Fifth revised edition 1972
Sixth revised edition 1973
Seventh revised edition 1974
Eighth revised edition 1976
Second impression 1976
Third impression 1977
Fourth impression 1978

Published by
THE HAMLYN PUBLISHING GROUP LIMITED
London ● New York ● Sydney ● Toronto
Astronaut House, Feltham, Middlesex, England

Printed in Italy
ISBN O 600 33126 1

CONTENTS

THE WORLD: USEFUL FACTS AND FIGURES

PEOPLE AND PLACES

PEOPLE AND THE NEW WORLD

PEOPLE ON THE MOVE

PEOPLE AND LANGUAGE

PEOPLE AND SCIENCE

PEOPLE AND THE ARTS

PEOPLE AND SPORT

PEOPLE AND LEISURE

9

THE WORLD:
USEFUL FACTS AND FIGURES

These tables of sizes, distances, heights and depths, numbers and locations of various things in the world we live in should help in settling many school and family arguments.

The diagram below shows how far the planets are from the Sun in millions of miles and kilometres:

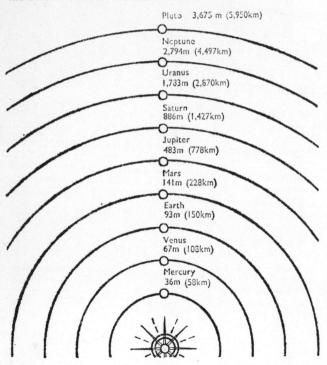

Pluto   3,675 m (5,950km)

Neptune
2,794m (4,497km)

Uranus
1,733m (2,870km)

Saturn
886m (1,427km)

Jupiter
483m (778km)

Mars
141m (228km)

Earth
93m (150km)

Venus
67m (108km)

Mercury
36m (58km)

The Solar System

The sun—the centre of our solar system—has a diameter of about 865,000 miles (1,392,000 km). The earth is one of nine planets which revolve round the sun. Here are these planets, together with some facts about them:

Planet	Diameter Miles	Diameter kilometres	One Revolution around Sun (days)	One Rotation on Axis
Mercury	3,008	4,840	88	88 days
Venus	7,600	12,300	225	not certain
Earth	7,927	12,756	365¼	23 h. 56 m.
Mars	4,200	6,790	687	24 h. 37 m.
Jupiter	88,439	134,700	4,332	9 h. 50 m.
Saturn	75,060	107,700	10,759	10 h. 14 m.
Uranus	30,875	47,100	30,687	10 h. 49 m.
Neptune	33,000	51,000	60,127	15 h. 40 m.
Pluto	3,600	5,900	90,400	unknown

The moon—the earth's satellite—has a diameter of 2,160 miles (3,476 km) and it is approximately 239,000 miles (385,000 km) away from the earth. Space flights to the moon have revealed no sign of life there, and no definite traces have been discovered on any of the planets—but studies point to possible life of some sort on Mars, probably in the vegetable category.

Land and Water

Much more than half the world's surface is ocean. In fact, the land area is only 55,786,000 square miles (143,500,000 square km) out of a total of 196,836,000 (508,500,000). The four great oceans are:

Name	Area (millions of sq. miles)	(millions of sq. km)
Pacific	64	165
Atlantic	31.5	81.5
Indian	28.35	73.5
Arctic	5.5	14.25

The six continents are:

Name	Area (millions of sq. miles)	(millions of sq. km)
Asia	17	44
Africa	11.7	30.3
North America	9	23.3
South America	7	18.1
Europe	3.8	9.8
Oceania	2.975	7.7

Ocean Deeps

Position	Name	Depth (feet)	(metres)
Mariana Trench	Challenger Deep	37,800	11,520
Tonga Trench	—	34,885	10,630
Philippine Trench	Galathea Deep	34,580	10,540
Kurile Trench	Vityaz Deep	34,045	10,375
Japanese Trench	Ramapo Deep	34,035	10,372
Kermadec Trench	—	32,788	9,995
Guam Trench	—	31,614	9,632
Puerto Rico Trench	Milwaukee Deep	30,246	9,200
New Britain Trench	Planet Deep	29,987	9,140

Great Seas and Lakes

Name and Location	Area (sq. miles)	(sq. km)
Mediterranean Sea (Southern Europe, Africa, Asia Minor)	1,100,000	2,850,000
South China Sea (China, East Indies)	960,000	2,486,000
Bering Sea (Alaska, Siberia)	878,000	2,274,000
Caribbean Sea (Central America, West Indies)	750,000	1,942,000
Gulf of Mexico (United States, Mexico)	716,000	1,855,000
Sea of Okhotsk (Siberia)	589,000	1,525,000
Hudson Bay (Canada)	475,000	1,230,000
Sea of Japan (Japan, U.S.S.R., Korea)	389,000	1,007,500
North Sea (North-western Europe)	221,000	572,400
Red Sea (Africa, Arabia)	178,000	461,000
Caspian Sea (U.S.S.R., Persia)	170,000	440,300
Black Sea (U.S.S.R., Turkey, Eastern Europe)	166,000	430,000
Baltic Sea (Scandinavia, U.S.S.R.)	163,000	422,000
Lake Superior (U.S.A., Canada)	31,820	82,400
Lake Victoria (East Central Africa)	26,820	69,480
Aral Sea (U.S.S.R.)	26,000	67,340
Lake Huron (U.S.A., Canada)	23,010	59,575
Lake Michigan (U.S.A.)	22,400	58,000
Lake Tanganyika (East Africa)	12,700	32,890

Large Islands

Name	Area (sq. miles)	(sq. km)
Greenland	840,000	2,175,600
New Guinea	345,000	893,500

Borneo	290,000	751,100
Madagascar	228,000	590,500
Baffin Land (Canada)	197,700	512,000
Sumatra	163,000	422,200
Great Britain	89,000	230,500
Honshu (Japan)	87,500	226,600
Ellesmere (Canada)	77,000	199,400
Celebes	72,500	187,800
South Island (New Zealand)	58,500	151,500
Java	48,400	125,400
North Island (New Zealand)	44,500	115,250
Cuba	44,000	114,000
Newfoundland (Canada)	42,750	110,700
Luzon (Philippine Islands)	41,000	106,200
Iceland	40,000	103,600

Great Rivers

Some of the longest rivers of the world are as follows:

River	Outflow	Length miles	kilometres
Nile	Mediterranean	4,160	6,695
Amazon	Atlantic	4,050	6,520
Missippi-Missouri-Red Rock	Gulf of Mexico	3,710	5,970
Yangtze	North Pacific	3,400	5,470
Yenisei	Arctic	3,300	5,310
Mekong	China Sea	2,800	4,500
Congo	Atlantic	2,710	4,375
Amur	North Pacific	2,700	4,345
Ob	Arctic	2,700	4,345
Lena	Arctic	2,680	4,310
Mackenzie	Beaufort Sea	2,635	4,240
Niger	Gulf of Guinea	2,600	4,185

Hwang-ho	North Pacific	2,600	4,185
Parana	Atlantic	2,450	3,940
Volga	Caspian Sea	2,290	3,685
Yukon	Bering Sea	1,979	3,185
St. Lawrence	Gulf of St. Lawrence	1,900	3,055
Rio Grande	Gulf of Mexico	1,885	3,035
São Francisco	Atlantic	1,800	2,895
Danube	Black Sea	1,770	2,850
Salween	Gulf of Martaban	1,700	2,735
Euphrates	Persian Gulf	1,700	2,735
Indus	Arabian Sea	1,700	2,735
Brahmaputra	Bay of Bengal	1,680	2,700
Zambezi	Indian Ocean	1,633	2,625

High Waterfalls

Some of the world's highest waterfalls (in a single leap) are as follows:

Falls	Country	Drop Feet	Metres
Angel	Venezuela	2,648	807
Cuquenan	Venezuela	2,000	610
Ribbon	U.S.A.	1,612	490
W. Mardalsfoss	Norway	1,535	467
Upper Yosemite	U.S.A.	1,430	436
Gavarnie	France	1,385	421
Tugela	South Africa	1,385	412
Glass	Brazil	1,325	403
Krimmi	Austria	1,250	381
Takkakaw	Canada	1,200	366
Silver Strand	U.S.A.	1,170	357
Geissbach	Switzerland	1,150	350
Wollomombie	Australia	1,100	335
Cusiana	Colombia	984	300

Staubbach	Switzerland	984	300
E. Mardalsfoss	Norway	974	297
Helena	New Zealand	890	271
Vetisfoss	Norway	889	271
Chirombo	Zambia	880	268

The famous Victoria Falls (Rhodesia, Zambia) has a drop of 355 feet (108 metres) and Niagara Falls (U.S.A., Canada) has a drop of 193 feet (59 metres).

Great Lakes

Some of the world's greatest lakes are as follows:

Lake	Location	Area Square miles	Square kilometres
Caspian Sea	Asia	170,000	440,300
Superior	North America	31,820	82,400
Victoria Nyanza	Africa	26,820	69,480
Aral	U.S.S.R.	26,000	67,340
Huron	North America	23,010	59,575
Michigan	North America	22,400	58,000
Tanganyika	Africa	12,700	32,890
Great Bear	Canada	12,200	31,600
Baikal	U.S.S.R.	12,150	31,470
Great Slave	Canada	11,170	28,930
Malawi	Africa	11,000	28,490
Erie	North America	9,940	25,740

Highest Mountains

Some of the World's highest mountains are as follows:

Mountain	Country	Height Feet	Metres
Everest	Nepal, Tibet	29,028	8,850
K2 (Godwin Austen)	Kashmir	28,250	8,610
Minya Konka	China	24,900	7,590
Aconcagna	Argentina	22,976	7,000
McKinley	Alaska	20,320	6,190
Logan	Canada	19,850	6,050
Kilimanjaro	Tanzania	19,340	5,890
Elbruz	U.S.S.R.	18,526	5,660
Mont Blanc	France	15,771	4,800
Ben Nevis	Scotland	4,406	1,340

Many other peaks in the Himalayas and Andes mountain ranges are nearly as high as Everest and Aconcagna but are not listed.

Natural Resources of the World

The pattern of modern civilisation is based upon what the earth can provide. Lands in which the earth is barren, or the climate too extreme, attract few people unless saleable minerals can be mined; but rich, fertile areas are usually densely populated. In the following paragraphs some of the staple needs of man are listed, with details of the areas in which they are found.

Meat and Dairy Produce. Most peoples of the world are meat eaters, and though cattle for meat can be raised on rough grassland, rich pasture is needed for dairy cattle, the source of milk, from which butter and cheese are made. The great beef-producing countries are the United States, Canada,

Argentina and Australia. The major dairying nations are New Zealand, Australia, the United States, Denmark and the Netherlands.

Sheep and Wool Produce. The big sheep-producing countries are Australia, New Zealand, Argentina and Russia. The ideal sheep for economic breeding is a cross between the English strain, raised for its tender meat, and the Merino, of Mediterranean breed, noted for its wool and leather.

Cereals. Man has been developing cereals from the original wild grasses of the world since he first began to cultivate the soil. The principal cereals are wheat, oats, barley, rice, rye and maize. The great wheat areas of the world are Canada, the United States, Argentina, Australia and Eastern Europe. Asia is the source of most of the world's rice.

Tea. Tea is grown mainly in India, China, Ceylon and Japan, with the greatest export trade being carried out by India, which sends millions of pounds in weight every year to the major tea-drinking countries.

Coffee. The coffee plant, which takes five years to grow to a crop-yielding size, is grown mainly in Brazil, Colombia and East Africa.

Cocoa. The cocoa bean was brought back to Europe from Central America in the fifteenth century, by the first explorers. Today the principal growing area is West Africa, which produces enormous quantities every year for making chocolate and cocoa powder.

Sugar. There are two sources of sugar. These are sugar cane and sugar beet. Sugar cane is a tropical plant of which the stems yield a syrupy juice. This is boiled to purify and crystallise it. The juice of the sugar beet, a vegetable grown in temperate climates, is refined in a similar way. The principal sugar cane area is the West Indies.

Tobacco. Grown wild by the natives of North America, tobacco was brought to Europe in the sixteenth century. The main plantations are in the southern United States, but tobacco is also grown extensively in Rhodesia and the

Middle East, and to a limited extent in many other areas for local use.

Cotton. Sub-tropical areas are best for cotton production, and the principal cotton countries are the United States, in its southern states, the West Indies, Egypt, India, China and southern Russia.

Rubber. Though some countries now produce much of their rubber by synthetic processes, rubber is still a major source of agricultural revenue for countries bordering the Equator. The main growing area embraces Malaysia, to which the original rubber trees were brought from Brazil, and nearby islands of Malaysia and Indonesia. Rubber is collected by cutting narrow grooves in the bark and allowing the natural rubber, or 'latex' to drip into a cup attached to the tree.

Minerals. Mineral ores are the source of the metals man needs, and most of them are found at considerable depth. Open-cast mining is used for surface lodes of minerals, but most mines are deep shafts with underground galleries penetrating hundreds of feet into the heart of the lode. Gold is found mainly in South Africa, Australia and North and South America. Copper and lead are found in every continent, silver in Central and South America and the Far East, and iron in most parts of the world. Uranium, the important metallic element used for atomic energy, is found mainly in the pitchblende deposits of the Congo and Canada.

Fuel. Coal, oil and natural gas are the fuels on which modern industrial society is based. Coal of varying quality is found in most parts of the world, and is extensively mined in Britain, Europe, the United States and the U.S.S.R. The great oil-producing countries are the United States, Canada, Venezuela and the Middle Eastern countries. Britain is expecting oil recently found in the North Sea to provide for much of her needs after 1980. Although only a small fraction of the world's oil and coal has been consumed, the demands of modern life are causing anxiety about when supplies will

19

eventually run out. Nuclear power is already being produced, and other possible sources of energy being developed are the heat of the earth (geothermal energy) and the heat of the sun (solar energy).

Fisheries. Sea fishing is carried on in all parts of the world, but the areas which produce more than is needed for local consumption are the Grand Banks of Newfoundland, famous for cod, the herring fisheries of Iceland and those streching southward as far as the Portuguese coast, and the salmon areas of the North Pacific.

PEOPLE AND PLACES

The First Men: Who were the first men? After a succession of ice ages lasting for hundreds of thousands of years, bleak millions of years in which the earth was inhabited by enormous reptiles, further ice ages, and also a long period dominated by early men, who had learned to use primitive tools and clothe themselves, the first true men seem to have emerged about fifty thousand years ago. They were hunters; they used spears and throwing-stones, wore skins and furs, and painted on the walls of their caves—paintings which remain to be seen today in caves in France and Spain.

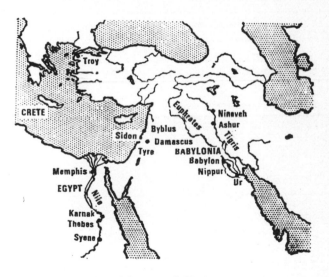

Early Centres of Civilisation

About eight thousand years ago, man had improved to a level at which he made finely polished stone implements, and cultivated fields of corn. Then, about six thousand years ago, came the first civilisations—in the Nile Valley, and in Mesopotamia between the Rivers Tigris and Euphrates. Empires and city-states spread across Arabia, into Turkey and thence to Europe; sailors made their first perilous journeys upon the Mediterranean, taking months of labour and danger to cover distances which a modern liner traverses between sunrise and dusk.

Empire followed empire—Egyptian, Greek, Roman, Chinese—and slowly men grouped themselves by race, religion and way of life into the nations of the present day, while the world's population rose from a few million to the present estimated total of some 4,000,000,000.

Countries of the World. The lists which follow cannot be completely accurate, as not all countries have been fully surveyed and not every area has a census of population, but they are reliable enough for most purposes, based on figures available at the time of going to press.

British Commonwealth

Country	Population (in Millions)	Capital	Population
Europe			
United Kingdom	54.500	London	7,200,000
Cyprus	0.633	Nicosia	117,000
Gibraltar	0.029	Gibraltar	20,000
Malta	0.317	Valletta	14,000
Asia			
Bangladesh	72.000	Dacca	1,300,000
Brunei	0.150	Bandar Seri Begawan	37,000

	Millions		
Hongkong	4.350	Victoria	767,000
India	550.000	Delhi	4,000,000
Malaysia	9.000	Kuala Lumpur	550,000
Singapore	2.220	—	
Sri Lanka	13.000	Colombo	562,000

Africa

Botswana	0.630	Gaborone	18,436
Gambia	0.493	Banjul	39,476
Ghana	8.545	Accra	633,800
Kenya	10.942	Nairobi	509,286
Lesotho	1.081	Maseru	30,000
Malawi	5.040	Lilongwe	—
Mauritius	0.834	Port Louis	140,000
Nigeria	80.000	Lagos	700,000
*Rhodesia	6.310	Salisbury	500,000
Sierra Leone	2.500	Freetown	128,000
Swaziland	0.465	Mbabane	14,000
Tanzania	15.000	Dar-es-Salaam	306,000
Uganda	11.172	Kampala	331,900
Zambia	4.751	Lusaka	415,000

North America

Canada	22.830	Ottawa	602,510

* Rhodesia declared unilateral independence on 11 November 1965

Central America and West Indies

	Millions		
Bahamas	0.194	Nassau	112,000
Barbados	0.243	Bridgetown	8,789
Belize	0.138	Belmopan	3,500
Bermuda	0.053	Hamilton	3,000
Grenada	0.106	St George's	6,313
Jamaica	2.025	Kingston	117,400
Trinidad and Tobago	1.062	Port of Spain	63,000

South America

Falkland Islands	0.002	Stanley	1,100
Guyana	0.794	Georgetown	168,000

Oceania

Australia	13.338	Canberra	198,000
Fiji	0.535	Suva	54,157
Gilbert and Ellice Islands	0.058	Tarawa	10,616
Nauru	0.007	Nauru	—
New Hebrides	0.086	Vila	5,500
New Zealand	3.105	Wellington	357,000
Papua New Guinea	2.500	Port Moresby	66,000
Samoa, Western	0.155	Apia	28,800
Solomon Islands	0.179	Honiara	17,000
Tonga	0.092	Nuku'alofa	20,000

Foreign Countries

Europe

Albania	2.400	Tirana	175,000
Andorra	0.020	Andorra La Vella	8,500

		Millions		
Austria	7.456	Vienna	1,614,341
Belgium	9.651	Brussels	1,055,000
Bulgaria	8.706	Sofia	946,305
Czechoslovakia	14.738	Prague	1,161,000
Denmark	5.054	Copenhagen	1,380,118
Finland	4.692	Helsinki	860,500
France	52.700	Paris	2,317,227
Germany, West	62.000	Bonn	283,000
Germany, East	17.000	East Berlin	1,088,828
Greece	8.769	Athens	2,540,240
Hungary	10.510	Budapest	2,047,000
Iceland	0.216	Reykjavik	84,772
Irish Republic	2.978	Dublin	567,861
Italy	54.137	Rome	2,842,616
Liechtenstein	0.024	Vaduz	4,380
Luxembourg	0.353	Luxembourg	78,032
Monaco	0.024	Monaco	2,422
Netherlands	13.600	Amsterdam	991,000
Norway	3.997	Oslo	468,337
Poland	33.800	Warsaw	1,388,000
Portugal	8.668	Lisbon	1,034,141
Romania	20.130	Bucharest	1,565,872
San Marino	0.019	San Marino	2,000
Spain	33.824	Madrid	3,146,070
Sweden	8.177	Stockholm	1,489,140
Switzerland	6.270	Berne	288,100
U.S.S.R. (Europe and Asia)	255.500	Moscow	7,734,000
Vatican City State	0.001	Vatican City	1,000
Yugoslavia	21.155	Belgrade	1,204,271
United Arab Emirates	0.656	Abu Dhabi	235,662

Asia

	Millions		
Afghanistan	16.900	Kabul	450,000
Bahrain	0.216	Manama	89,728
Bhutan	1.100	Thinphu	
Burma	28.870	Rangoon	3,662,312
China	800.000	Peking	000,000,8
Indonesia	132.000	Djakarta	4,600,000
Iran	33.000	Tehran	3,150,000
Iraq	11.120	Baghdad	3,000,000
Israel	3.400	Jerusalem	344,200
Japan	110.050	Tokyo	11,701,899
Kampuchea	6.800	Phnom Penh	
Korea, South	34.688	Seoul	8,684,000
Kuwait	0.990	Kuwait	300,000
Laos	2.900	Vientiane	176,637
Lebanon	2.780	Beirut	702,000
Mongolia (Outer)	1.380	Ulan Bator	282,000
Nepal	11.700	Katmandu	195,000
Oman	0.750	Muscat	7,650
Pakistan	66.749	Islamabad	235,000
Philippine Islands	42.517	Manila	4,500,000
Qatar	0.180	Doha	130,000
Saudi Arabia	8.697	Riyadh	350,000
Syria	6.800	Damascus	836,668
Thailand	39.950	Bangkok	4,300,000
Turkey (Asia and Europe)	39.066	Ankara	1,236,152
Socialist Republic of Vietnam	43.787	Hanoi	1,378,335
Yemen	7.000	San'a	125,000
Yemen P.D.R.	1.590	Aden	250,000

26

Africa

	Millions		
Algeria	14.600	Algiers	1,000,000
Angola	5.673	St. Paul de Luanda	346,763
Benin	2.948	Porto Novo	100,000
Burundi	3.500	Bujumbura	100,000
Cameroon	6.400	Yaoundé	180,000
Cape Verde Islands	0.272	Praia	6,000
Central African Empire	2.255	Bangui	301,793
Chad	3.869	N'djamena	192,962
Congo	1.300	Brazzaville	289,700
Egypt	37.600	Cairo	8,143,000
Equatorial Guinea	0.300	Malabo	20,000
Ethiopia	26.461	Addis Ababa	912,000
Gabon	0.950	Libreville	75,000
Guinea	3.890	Conakry	120,000
Guinea Bissau	0.570	Bissau	65,000
Ivory Coast	5.700	Abidjan	500,000
Liberia	1.500	Monrovia	180,000
Libya	2.260	Tripoli	376,170
Madagascar	7.185	Tananarive	382,000
Mali	5.600	Bamako	170,000
Mauritania	1.240	Nouakchott	70,000
Morocco	16.310	Rabat	702,600
Mozambique	8.233	Maputo	800,000
Niger	4.239	Niamey	102,000
Reunion	0.476	St-Denis	90,000
Rwanda	5.500	Kigali	7,000
Senegal	4.100	Dakar	581,000
Somalia	2.930	Mogadiscio	350,000

South Africa	21.402	Pretoria	561,703
		Cape Town	1,096,597
Sudan	12.428	Khartoum	228,000
Togo	2.198	Lomé	135,000
Tunisia	5.270	Tunis	784,787
Upper Volta	5.870	Ouagadougou	124,779
Zaire	24.800	Kinshasa	2,200,000

Central America and West Indies
Millions

Costa Rica	1.872	San José	720,894
Cuba	9.170	Havana	1,735,360
Dominican			
Republic	4.000	Santo Domingo	822,862
Guadeloupe	0.334	Basse-Terre	15,690
Guatemala	5.200	Guatemala	717,322
Haiti	4.450	Port au Prince	500,000
Honduras	2.800	Tegucigalpa	274,850
Martinique	0.339	Fort de France	99,051
Nicaragua	2.210	Managua	318,000
Panama	1.678	Panama City	442,000
Puerto Rico	2.712	San Juan	455,421
(El) Salvador	3.712	San Salvador	340,000
Virgin Islands		Charlotte	
(U.S.)	0.063	Amalie	13,000

North America

Mexico	56.240	Mexico City	8,941,912
United States	213.631	Washington	
		D.C.	2,861,123

South America

	Millions		
Argentina	23.390	Buenos Aires	8,774,529
Bolivia	5.639	La Paz	697,000
Brazil	93.139	Brasilia	537,500
Chile	10.405	Santiago	3,700,000
Colombia	23.950	Bogotá	2,978,300
Ecuador	6.500	Quito	557,113
Guiana, French	0.049	Cayenne	24,581
Paraguay	2.354	Asunción	392,753
Peru	15.400	Lima	3,600,000
Surinam	0.385	Paramaribo	102,300
Uruguay	2.764	Montevideo	1,229,748
Venezuela	11.500	Caracas	1,860,000

	Oceania		
French Polynesia	0.120	Papeete	79,494
New Caledonia	0.132	Noumea	59,869

The World's Largest Cities

Name	Population
Tokyo, Japan	11,701,899
Shanghai, China	10,000,000
Mexico City, Mexico	8,941,912
Buenos Aires, Argentina	8,774,529
Seoul, Korea	8,684,000
Cairo, Egypt	8,143,000
Peking, China	8,000,000
New York, U.S.A.	7,895,563
Moscow, U.S.S.R.	7,734,000
London, England	7,200,000
Tientsin, China	7,000,000

Chungking, China	6,000,000
Sao Paulo, Brazil	5,901,533
Bombay, India	5,850,000
Canton, China	5,000,000
Shenyang, China	4,400,000
Leningrad, U.S.S.R.	4,372,000
Bangkok, Thailand	4,300,000
Rio de Janeiro, Brazil	4,296,782
Luta, China	4,200,000
Delhi, India	4,065,698
Santiago, Chile	4,000,000
Lima, Peru	3,600,000
Chicago, U.S.A.	3,369,357
Rangoon, Burma	3,186,886
Tehran, Iran	3,150,000
Madrid, Spain	3,146,070
Calcutta, India	3,141,180
Berlin, Germany (East & West)	3,078,984
Sydney, Australia	3,021,300
Rome, Italy	2,842,616
Los Angeles, U.S.A.	2,809,813
Athens, Greece	2,540,240
Paris, France	2,317,227

The World's Tallest Buldings

The highest buildings in England are:
Post Office Tower, London—580 ft (177 m)
Salisbury Cathedral (spire)—404 ft (123 m)
St. Paul's Cathedral (cross), London—365 ft (111 m)

The tallest tower in the world is at Ostankino, near Moscow, U.S.S.R. With its television antennae it reaches 1,762 feet (537 m). It has a 3-storey restaurant revolving near the top.

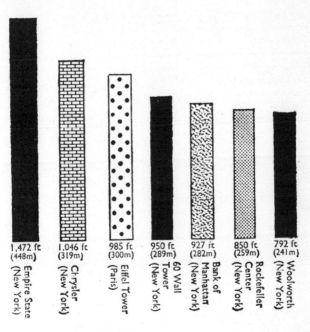

1,472 ft (448m) Empire State (New York)

1,046 ft (319m) Chrysler (New York)

985 ft (300m) Eiffel Tower (Paris)

950 ft (289m) 60 Wall Tower (New York)

927 ft (282m) Bank of Manhattan (New York)

850 ft (259m) Rockefeller Center (New York)

792 ft (241m) Woolworth (New York)

The Seven Wonders of the World

It would be a hard task for anyone to name the Seven Wonders of the Modern World, but certainly among the candidates would be space travel, nuclear power, the jet engine, television, radar and some of the almost miraculous discoveries of recent years in medicine.

The Seven Wonders of the Ancient World were:

The Pyramids of Egypt, of which the biggest, the Great Pyramid of Cheops, was originally more than 480 feet (146 m) in height.

The Hanging Gardens of Babylon, near Baghdad. These were terraced gardens, irrigated by means of huge storage tanks on the uppermost terraces.

The Tomb of Mausolus at Halicarnassus, in Asia Minor.

The Temple of Diana (Artemis) at Ephesus, a great marble temple dating from c. 350 B.C.

The Statue of Jupiter (Zeus) at Olympia, built of marble and inlaid with gold about 430 B.C.

The Colossus of Rhodes, a bronze statue, about 105 feet (32 m) high, with its legs astride the harbour entrance at Rhodes.

The Pharos at Alexandria, the world's first real lighthouse.

Religions of the World

There remain well over 1,000 million of the world's population unclassified, because their religion is either unknown, or they have no religion, or because they follow primitive, tribal or other religions or beliefs.

Religions of the World

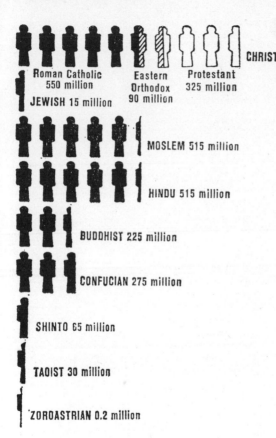

CHRISTIAN 965 million

Roman Catholic 550 million

Eastern Orthodox 90 million

Protestant 325 million

JEWISH 15 million

MOSLEM 515 million

HINDU 515 million

BUDDHIST 225 million

CONFUCIAN 275 million

SHINTO 65 million

TAOIST 30 million

ZOROASTRIAN 0.2 million

Great Dates in History

B.C.

c. 3400	First Egyptian Dynastic Period
2900	The Great Pyramid of Egypt built by Cheops
1300	Phoenicians open up Mediterranean trade
1230	Exodus of the Israelites from Egypt
1190	Fall of Troy
961	Building of the Temple at Jerusalem begun
776	First Olympic Games held in Greece
753	Founding of Rome
490	Greeks defeat Persians at Marathon
488	Death of Buddha
335-23	The campaigns of Alexander the Great
146	Carthage destroyed by Scipio
55	Julius Caesar invades Britain
4	Actual date of the birth of Christ

A.D.

30	Crucifixion
43	Conquest of Britain by Rome begun
70	Destruction of Jerusalem
79	Vesuvius erupts, destroying Pompeii and Herculaneum
122	Building of Hadrian's Wall
407	Romans leave Britain
476	Fall of the Roman Empire in the West
569	Birth of Mohammed in Mecca
711	Moors overrun Spain
732	Moors driven from France
1000	Norsemen reach Labrador
1066	Normans conquer Britain
1095	The Crusades begin
1215	The Magna Carta sealed by King John
1216	First Parliament in England
1271	Beginning of Marco Polo's travels
1338	Hundred Years War begins

1348	The Black Death sweeps Europe
1440	Printing with movable type begun in Germany
1453	Eastern Roman Empire falls to Turks
1455–85	Wars of the Roses
1476	First printing press in England
1492	Columbus discovers America
1492	Moors driven from Spain
1500	Portuguese discover Brazil
1519–22	First voyage round the world, by Magellan
1534	Reformation in England
1536	Dissolution of the monasteries in England
1572	Massacre of St. Bartholomew in France
1577–80	Drake's voyage round the world
1588	Drake defeats Spanish Armada
1605	Gunpowder Plot to blow up English Parliament
1607	First permanent colony established in Virginia
1618–48	Thirty Years War
1620	*Mayflower* colonists land in New England
1642	New Zealand and Tasmania discovered
1665	Great Plague of London
1666	Great Fire of London
1707	Act of Union unites England and Scotland
1715	First Jacobite Rebellion
1745	Second Jacobite Rebellion, 'The Forty-five'
1756	Beginning of Seven Years War
1760	British defeat French in Canada
c. 1760	Beginning of Industrial Revolution
1770	Captain Cook discovers New South Wales
1775–83	American War of Independence
1776	American Declaration of Independence
1789	French Revolution begins
1796	Napoleonic Wars begin
1804	Napoleon becomes Emperor of France
1805	Battle of Trafalgar
1815	Battle of Waterloo
1832	First Reform Act in Parliament

1833	Britain abolishes slavery
1840	Introduction of penny post in Britain
1848	Gold discovered in California
1854–56	Crimean War
1857	Indian Mutiny
1861–65	American Civil War
1863	United States abolishes slavery
1867	Dominion of Canada established
1869	Suez Canal opens
1870–71	Franco-Prussian War
1877–78	Russo-Turkish War breaks power of Turkey in Europe
1899–02	Boer War
1903	First successful aeroplane flight, by Wright brothers
1904–05	Russo-Japanese War
1909	Blériot makes first cross-Channel flight
1909	Peary reaches North Pole
1911	Amundsen reaches South Pole
1912	Ocean liner *Titanic* sinks, 1,513 lost
1914	World War I begins
1915	Ocean liner *Lusitania* torpedoed, 1,500 lost
1917	United States enters World War I
1917	Russian Revolution
1918	End of World War I
1919	Alcock and Brown make first non-stop trans-Atlantic flight
1920	First meeting of League of Nations
1922	Mussolini marches on Rome
1924	Death of Lenin
1926	General Strike takes place in Britain
1927	Lindbergh makes first solo flight across Atlantic
1929	Start of the Great Slump
1931	Japan occupies Manchuria
1933	Hitler attains power in Germany
1935	Italy invades Ethiopia

1936–39	Civil War in Spain
1937	Japan begins war on China
1938	Germany annexes Austria, Munich Agreement
1939	Outbreak of World War II
1940	Germany invades Denmark, Norway, Netherlands, Belgium and Luxembourg
1940	Dunkirk evacuation. Paris taken by Germans
1940	Battle of Britain
1941	Russia and United States enter World War II
1942	All of France occupied by Germans
1943	Russians halt German advance at Stalingrad
1943	Allies invade Italy
1944	Allies invade France
1945	Germany surrenders. Hitler dies
1945	First atomic bomb dropped on Japan
1945	End of World War II
1945	Japan surrenders
1945	United Nations established
1947	India attains independence
1948	State of Israel proclaimed
1950–53	Korean War
1953	Conquest of Mount Everest
1956	Suez Canal dispute
1957	Russians launch first space satellites
1959	Russians launch first rocket to reach moon and photograph its far side
1960	Piccard descends 7 miles under the Pacific
1961	First space flight, by Yuri Gagarin
1963	Assassination of President Kennedy
1964	Pope Paul VI visits the Holy Land and becomes first reigning Pope to travel by air
1965	Death of Sir Winston Churchill
1966	River Arno overflows and floods two-thirds of the City of Florence, Italy
1967	China explodes complete H-bomb
1969	Neil Amstrong first man on the moon

1971	Indo-Pakistan conflict. East Pakistan becomes Bangladesh
1971	China admitted to the United Nations
1974	President Nixon resigns after impeachment proceedings
1975	End of Vietnam War

Exploration and Discoveries of the Past Years

1497	East coast of Canada, by John Cabot
1498	Cape route to India, by Vasco da Gama
1498	South America, by Christopher Columbus
1513	Pacific Ocean, by Vasco Nuñez de Balboa
1519	Magellan Strait, by Ferdinand Magellan
1534	St. Lawrence River, by Jacques Cartier
1605–06	Australia, by Willem Jansz
1610	Hudson Bay (Canada), by Henry Hudson
1616	Baffin Bay (Canada), by William Baffin
1642	New Zealand and Tasmania, by Abel Janszoon Tasman
1778	Hawaii, by James Cook
1820	Antarctic mainland, by Edward Bransfield
1855	Victoria Falls, by David Livingstone
1858	Source of the Nile, by John Hanning Speke
1865	Matterhorn summit first reached, by Edward Whymper
1909	North Pole first reached, by Robert E. Peary
1911	South Pole first reached, by Roald Amundsen
1958	American atomic-powered submarine *Nautilus* makes first undersea crossing beneath the North Pole ice cap in 96 hours
1965	Alexei Leonov becomes the first man to walk in space
1966	Russian Space probe achieves first soft landing on the Moon
1969	Neil Armstrong and Edwin Aldrin become the first men to land on the Moon

1971   New peak in American Space Programme reached as U.S. astronauts drive 'Lunar-Rover' across Moon's surface

The United Nations

There has seldom, if ever, been a year without war in some quarter of the globe. In 1944, towards the end of World War II, a conference was held at Washington between statesmen of Britain, China, the Soviet Union and the United States—the four 'Great Powers' on the Allied side in the War—to plan a world-wide organisation of countries pledged to prevent war (successor to the League of Nations). The first full meeting of the United Nations was held in 1945, at San Francisco, and the building of the present headquarters, in New York, was begun soon afterwards. The 147 members of the United Nations are:

Afghanistan	Canada	Fiji
Albania	Cape Verde	Finland
Angola	Central African	France
Australia	Empire	Gabon
Austria	Chad	Gambia
Bahamas	Chile	Germany (East)
Bahrain	China	Germany (West)
Bangladesh	Colombia	Ghana
Barbados	Congo	Grenada
Belgium	Cormoros	Greece
Benin	Costa Rica	Guatemala
Bhutan	Cuba	Guinea
Bolivia	Cyprus	Guinea Bissau
Botswana	Czechoslovakia	Guyana
Brazil	Denmark	Haiti
Bulgaria	Dominican Rep.	Honduras
Burma	Ecuador	Hungary
Burundi	Egypt	Iceland
Byelorussian S.S.R.	Equatorial Guinea	
Cameroon	Ethiopia	

India
Indonesia
Iran
Iraq
Irish Republic
Israel
Italy
Ivory Coast
Jamaica
Japan
Kampuchea
Kuwait
Laos
Lebanon
Lesotho
Liberia
Libya
Luxembourg
Madagascar
Malawi
Malaysia
Maldive
 Islands
Mali
Malta
Mauritania
Mauritius
Mexico

Mongolian P.R.
Mozambique
Netherlands
New Zealand
Nicaragua
Niger
Nigeria
Norway
Oman
Pakistan
Panama
Papua New Guinea
Paraguay
Peru
Philippines
Poland
Portugal
Qatar
Romania
Rwanda
(El) Salvador
Sao Tomé
and Principe
Seychelles
Sierra Leone
Singapore
Somalia
South Africa

Spain
Sri Lanka
Surinam
Sweden
Tanzania
Togo
Trinidad and
 Tobago
Tunisia
Turkey
Uganda
Ukrainian S.S.R.
Ukraine
U.S.S.R.
United Arab
 Emirates
United Kingdom
United States
Upper Volta
Uruguay
Venezuela
Yemen
Yemen (P.D.R.)
Yugoslavia
Zaire
Zambia

The General Assembly consists of all members. Any important issue brought before it is settled by a two-thirds majority vote; lesser issues require only a simple majority. The Security Council is made up of fifteen members and is in continuous session to prevent international disputes. There are five permanent members: United Kingdom, United States, U.S.S.R., France and China. The General Assembly chooses the remaining members, electing them for a period of two years. The Council reaches procedure decisions by an affirmative vote of nine members, but in other matters five of the votes must be those of the permanent members. If any one of these members votes against the majority, this vote is in effect a veto, and no settlement can be reached.

There are four other sections of the United Nations: the Economic and Social Council, the Trusteeship Council, the International Court of Justice and the Secretariat.

The United Nations also runs various agencies. These are as follows: International Atomic Energy Agency (I.A.E.A.), International Labour Organization (I.L.O.), Food and Agriculture Organization of the United Nations (F.A.O.), United Nations Educational Scientific and Cultural Organization (U.N.E.S.C.O.), World Health Organization (W.H.O.), International Monetary Fund, International Bank for Reconstruction and Development (The World Bank), International Finance Corporation (I.F.C.), International Civil Aviation Organization (I.C.A.O.), International Telecommunication Union (I.T.U.), World Meteorological Organization (W.M.O.), Inter-governmental Maritime Consultative Organization (I.M.C.O.), General Agreement on Tariffs and Trade (G.A.T.T.).

Other Alliances

Apart from the United Nations, countries have found it necessary or advantageous to form other alliances either for defence or trade purposes. Some of the most important are as follows:

European Economic Community (E.E.C., called the Common Market). The community was formed on 1 January 1958 to promote closer union and co-operation between European countries mainly for trade purposes. The founder members were Belgium, France, Germany, Italy, Luxembourg and the Netherlands. The United Kingdom, the Irish Republic and Denmark became members on 1 January 1973.

North Atlantic Treaty Organization (N.A.T.O.). This was formed in 1949 to settle by peaceful means any international disputes in which member nations might be involved. The founder members were Belgium, Canada, Denmark, France, Iceland, Italy, Luxembourg, the Netherlands, Norway, Portugal, U.K. and U.S.A. Later members were Greece, Turkey and West Germany.

South East Asia Collective Defence Treaty. A pact made in 1954 to establish a collective defence system in South-East Asia between Australia, France, New Zealand, Pakistan, the Philippines, Thailand, U.K. and U.S.A.

Central Treaty Organization (C.E.N.T.O.). A pact of mutual defence signed by Turkey and Iraq in 1955 and joined by U.K., Pakistan, Iran and U.S.A. Iraq withdrew in 1959. The pact was originally known as the Baghdad Pact.

Monarchs of the World

Almost all countries of the world today have a parliamentary system—that is, a council of people elected to rule.

By far the majority of nations have at their head a President, in most cases elected every few years. Those which still have hereditary monarchs are:

Country	Ruler	Came to Throne
Belgium	King Baudouin	1951
Denmark	Queen Margrethe II	1972
Great Britain	Queen Elizabeth II	1952
Iran	Shah Mohammed Reza Pahlevi	1941
Japan	Emperor Hirohito	1926
Jordan	King Hussein	1952
Liechtenstein	Prince Francis Joseph II	1938
Luxembourg	Grand Duke Jean	1964
Monaco	Prince Rainier III	1949
Morocco	King Hassan II	1961

Nepal	Maharajadhiraja Birendra	
	Bir Bikram Shah Dev	1972
Netherlands	Queen Juliana	1948
Norway	King Olav V	1957
Saudi Arabia	King Khaled ibn Abdul Aziz	1975
Spain	King Juan Carlos I	1975
Sweden	King Carl Gustaf	1973
Thailand	King Bhumibol Adulaydej	1946

The British Commonwealth of Nations

This is a free and equal association of the following nations: The United Kingdom, Australia, Bangladesh, Bahamas, Barbados, Bermuda, Botswana, British Honduras, Brunei, Canada, Cayman, Turks and Caicos Islands, Cyprus, Falkland Islands, Fiji, Gambia, Ghana, Gibraltar, Gilbert and Ellice Islands, Guyana, Hong Kong, India, Jamaica, Kenya, Lesotho, Malawi, Malaysia, Malta, Mauritius, Nauru, New Hebrides, New Zealand, Nigeria, Pitcairn, St Helena, Seychelles, Sierra Leone, Singapore, Solomon Islands, Sri Lanka, Swaziland, Tanzania, Tonga, Trinidad and Tobago, Uganda, Western Samoa, Zambia, Rhodesia. The Queen is Head of the Commonwealth but only remains Head of State in certain instances.

The Royal Family

Her Majesty Queen Elizabeth II succeeded her father, King George VI, at his death on February 6, 1952. Her Coronation was on June 2, 1953. She was born on April 21, 1926, and on November 20, 1947, she married Prince Philip, son of Prince Andrew of Greece. Prince Philip, Duke of Edinburgh, was born on June 10, 1921. Their eldest son, Prince Charles Philip Arthur George, Prince of Wales, the on August 15, 1950, and on November 14, 1973, was married to Capt. Mark Anthony Peter Phillips, C.V.O., and has one son, Peter Mark Andrew, born on November 15, 1977. Their second son, Prince Andrew Albert Christian Edward, was born on February 19, 1960. Their third son, Prince Edward Antony Richard Louis, was born on March 10, 1964.

The other immediate members of the Royal Family are: Queen Elizabeth the Queen Mother, born August 4, 1900, widow of the late King George VI; Princess Margaret Rose, sister of the Queen, born August 21, 1930.

The initial order of succession to the throne is: The Prince of Wales; Prince Andrew; Prince Edward; Princess Anne and her son; Princess Margaret and her son and daughter; The Duke of Gloucester; The Duke of Kent and his sons and daughter; Prince Michael of Kent; Princess Alexandra and her son and daughter.

Kings and Queens of England

Name		Born	Reign	
Saxons and Danes			*From*	*To*
Egbert	*c.*	775	827	839
Ethelwulf		—	839	858
Ethelbald		—	858	860
Ethelbert		—	860	866
Ethelred I		—	866	871
Alfred the Great	*c.*	849	871	900
Edward the Elder	*c.*	870	900	924
Athelstan	*c.*	895	924	940
Edmund I	*c.*	921	940	946
Edred	*c.*	925	946	955
Edwy	*c.*	943	955	959
Edgar		944	959	975
Edward the Martyr	*c.*	963	975	978
Ethelred II, the Unready	*c.*	968	978	1016
Edmund II, Ironside	*c.*	980	1016	1016
Canute		994	1017	1035
Harold I	*c.*	1016	1035	1040
Hardicanute	*c.*	1018	1040	1042

Edward the Confessor	*c.* 1004	1042	1066
Harold II	*c.* 1020	1066	1066

House of Normandy

William I	1027	1066	1087
William II	1057	1087	1100
Henry I	1068	1100	1135
Stephen, Count of Blois	1104	1135	1154

House of Plantagenet

Henry II	1133	1154	1189
Richard I	1157	1189	1199
John	1166	1199	1216
Henry III	1207	1216	1272
Edward I	1239	1272	1307
Edward II	1284	1307	1327
Edward III	1312	1327	1377
Richard II	1367	1377	1399
Henry IV ⎫	1366	1399	1413
Henry V ⎬ *Lancaster*	1388	1413	1422
Henry VI ⎭	1421	1422	1461
Edward IV ⎫	1442	1461	1483
Edward V ⎬ *York*	1470	1483	1483
Richard III ⎭	1452	1483	1485

House of Tudor

Henry VII	1457	1485	1509
Henry VIII	1491	1509	1547
Edward VI	1537	1547	1553
Jane (Lady Jane Grey)—9 days	1537	1553	1553
Mary I	1516	1553	1558
Elizabeth I	1533	1558	1603

House of Stuart

James I (VI of Scotland)	1566	1603	1625
Charles I	1600	1625	1649

Commonwealth created May 19, 1649, causing Interregnum

Oliver Cromwell (Lord Protector)	1599	1653	1658

Richard Cromwell (Lord Protector)	1626	1658	1659

House of Stuart (Restoration)

Charles II	1630	1660	1685
James II	1633	1685	1688
William III ⎫ *joint sovereigns*	1650	1689 ⎧	1702
Mary II ⎭	1662	⎨	1694
Anne	1665	1702	1714

House of Hanover

George I	1660	1714	1727
George II	1683	1727	1760
George III	1738	1760	1820
George IV	1762	1820	1830
William IV	1765	1830	1837
Victoria	1819	1837	1901

House of Saxe-Coburg

Edward VII	1841	1901	1910

House of Windsor

George V	1865	1910	1936
Edward VIII—325 days	1894	1936	1936
George VI	1895	1936	1952
Elizabeth II	1926	1952	—

Kings and Queens of Scotland

Name	Reign	
	From	*To*
Malcolm III (Canmore)	1057	1093
Donald I	1093	1094
Duncan II	1094	1094
Donald I (restored)	1094	1097
Edgar	1097	1107
Alexander I	1107	1124
David I	1124	1153

Malcolm IV (the Maiden)	1153	1165
William I (the Lion)	1165	1214
Alexander II	1214	1249
Alexander III	1249	1286
Margaret (Maid of Norway)	1286	1290
John Baliol	1292	1296
Robert I (Bruce)	1306	1329
David II	1329	1371
Robert II (Stewart)	1371	1390
Robert III	1390	1406
James I	1406	1437
James II	1437	1460
James III	1460	1488
James IV	1488	1513
James V	1513	1542
Mary (Queen of Scots)	1542	1587
James VI (became James I of England in 1603)	1567	1625

Royal Salutes

A Royal Salute of sixty-two guns is fired at the Tower of London each year on the anniversaries of the Queen's Birth, Accession to the Throne and Coronation. Forty-one guns are fired when the Queen opens or dissolves Parliament in person, when she passes through London in procession, and on the birth of a Royal child.

The Union Jack

The Union Jack is a flag composed of three crosses. These are the crosses of St. Andrew (white on blue), St. Patrick (red on white) and St. George (red on white). The first two are diagonal, the third vertical and horizontal. At the time it was adopted (1606) the flag contained only the crosses of St. George and St. Andrew, as it signified the accession of

The Royal Standard

James VI of Scotland to the English Throne as James I. The cross of St. Patrick (Ireland) was introduced when the Act of Union came into force in the year 1800. The flag is flown on government and public buildings in the United Kingdom, England, Scotland or Greater London (according to the event) on a number of Royal anniversaries and other important occasions, such as St. George's Day in England and St. Andrew's Day in Scotland, Remembrance Sunday, and at the special command of Her Majesty. It is flown at half-mast as a mark of respect when the death takes place of the Sovereign, Prime Minister and other important personages at home or abroad.

The Royal Standard

The Royal Standard is the personal flag of the Queen and is flown only on buildings in which the Queen is actually present, never when Her Majesty is passing in procession. It is divided into four quarters. In the first and fourth are the three lions passant of England; in the second appears the lion rampant of Scotland; in the third, the harp of Ireland.

The White, Red and Blue Ensigns

The White Ensign, bearing the cross of St. George on a white background, with the Union Jack filling the upper corner nearest the flagstaff, is the flag of the Royal Navy and the Royal Yacht Squadron.

The Red Ensign (the Red Duster) is a red flag with the Union Jack filling the upper corner nearest the flagstaff. It is flown by British merchant vessels.

The Blue Ensign is a blue flag with the Union Jack in the upper corner nearest the flagstaff. It is flown by the Royal Naval Reserve and by certain selected yacht clubs.

British Parliamentary Government

The Queen, though Head of the British Commonwealth, takes a purely formal part in government, which is carried on in each Commonwealth nation by a Prime Minister, and/or President, and his Cabinet, usually drawn from the membership of its Parliament. The Queen opens Parliament in Britain by making a speech from the Throne in the House of Lords, and the same ceremony has been carried out by Her Majesty in Commonwealth nations—though, as she is normally resident in Britain, this is usually the task of the Governor-General, who is the Queen's representative in those countries that recognise Her Majesty as Head of State. Other Commonwealth countries (Republics, etc.) have a High Commissioner in place of a Governor-General.

The method of government—usually parliamentary—varies considerably from one Commonwealth country to the next, but the pattern is generally based upon that of Britain, where the Cabinet consists of about nineteen Ministers. The head of the Cabinet is the Prime Minister, whose appointment is made personally by the Queen on the recommendation of 'elder statesmen'—senior politicians with a long record in public life.

Britain's Prime Ministers and changes of administration

Date	Name	Party
1721	Sir Robert Walpole	Whig
1742	Earl of Wilmington	Whig
1743	Henry Pelham	Whig
1754	Duke of Newcastle	Whig
1756	Duke of Devonshire	Whig
1757	Duke of Newcastle	Whig
1761	Earl of Bute	Tory
1763	George Grenville	Whig
1765	Marquess of Rockingham	Whig
1766	Earl of Chatham	Whig
1767	Duke of Grafton	Whig
1770	Lord North	Tory
1782	Marquess of Rockingham	Whig
1782	Earl of Shelburne	Whig
1783	Duke of Portland	Coalition

50

1783	William Pitt	Tory
1801	Henry Addington	Tory
1804	William Pitt	Tory
1806	Lord Grenville	Whig
1807	Duke of Portland	Tory
1809	Spender Perceval	Tory
1812	Earl of Liverpool	Tory
1827	George Canning	Tory
1827	Viscount Goderich	Tory
1828	Duke of Wellington	Tory
1830	Earl Grey	Whig
1834	Viscount Melbourne	Whig
1834	Sir Robert Peel	Tory
1835	Viscount Melbourne	Whig
1841	Sir Robert Peel	Tory
1846	Lord John Russell	Whig
1852	Earl of Derby	Tory
1852	Earl of Aberdeen	Peelite
1855	Viscount Palmerston	Liberal
1858	Earl of Derby	Conservative
1859	Viscount Palmerston	Liberal
1865	Lord John Russell	Liberal
1866	Earl of Derby	Conservative
1868	Benjamin Disraeli	Conservative
1868	William E. Gladstone	Liberal
1874	Benjamin Disraeli	Conservative
1880	William E. Gladstone	Liberal
1885	Marquess of Salisbury	Conservative
1886	William E. Gladstone	Liberal
1886	Marquess of Salisbury	Conservative
1892	William E. Gladstone	Liberal
1894	Earl of Rosebery	Liberal
1895	Marquess of Salisbury	Conservative
1902	A. J. Balfour	Conservative
1905	Sir H. Campbell-Bannerman	Liberal
1908	Herbert Asquith	Liberal

1915	Herbert Asquith	Coalition
1916	David Lloyd George	Coalition
1922	Andrew Bonar Law	Conservative
1923	Stanley Baldwin	Conservative
1924	J. Ramsay MacDonald	Labour
1924	Stanley Baldwin	Conservative
1929	J. Ramsay MacDonald	Labour
1931	J. Ramsay MacDonald	Coalition
1935	Stanley Baldwin	Coalition
1937	Neville Chamberlain	Coalition
1940	Winston Churchill	Coalition
1945	Clement R. Attlee	Labour
1951	Sir Winston Churchill	Conservative
1955	Sir Anthony Eden	Conservative
1957	Harold Macmillan	Conservative
1963	Sir Alec Douglas-Home	Conservative
1964	Harold Wilson	Labour
1970	Edward Heath	Conservative
1974	Harold Wilson	Labour
1976	James Callaghan	Labour

Some Principal Government Departments of the United Kingdom

Agriculture, Fisheries and Food. Farming, fishing, the maintenance and improvement of food supplies, and animal health. (Minister of Agriculture, Fisheries and Food)

Defence. The overall responsibility for national defence by the co-ordination of air, naval and military preparedness. (Secretary of State for Defence)

Education and Science. The organisation of the State educational system, from primary schools to universities and adult education. (Secretary of State for Education and Science)

Employment. All matters concerned with employment. (Secretary of State for Employment)

Environment. All matters concerning the environment. (Secretary of State for the Environment)

Foreign and Commonwealth Affairs. All matters relating to foreign and Commonwealth countries. (Secretary of State for Foreign and Commonwealth Affairs)

Health and Social Security. The running of the National Health Service. All matters concerning medicine, nursing, hospitals and public hygiene. The administration of insurance, family allowances, widows' and retirement pensions. (Secretary of State for Social Services)

Home Office. Law enforcement. The control of fire, police, prison and immigration services. (Secretary of State for the Home Department)

Scottish Office. All matters of particular concern to Scotland. (Secretary of State for Scotland)

Trade and Industry. Matters affecting British industry and trade, other than those handled by the Ministers of Agriculture, Fisheries and Food; and the Environment. (Secretary of State for Trade and Industry)

Transport Industries. Road, rail and sea transport of people and goods. (Minister for Transport Industries)

Treasury. All matters relating to finance and the national budget. Chancellor of the Exchequer)

Welsh Office. All matters of particular concern to Wales. (Secretary of State for Wales)

How Laws are Made and Who Makes Them

New laws are discussed and voted upon in the two Houses of Parliament. The House of Lords, presided over by the Lord High Chancellor, has a membership of about one thousand, comprising Royal princes, archbishops, dukes, marquesses, earls, viscounts, bishops, barons, life peers and law lords. The House of Commons, directed by the Speaker, is an elected assembly of 635 men and women (previously 630) who are paid an annual salary for attendance. Each represents a constituency (area of the country) which elected him or her by majority vote at the last General

Election, or a later By-election caused by the death or retirement of the previous representative. The normal span of a Parliament is five years, though at any time the Queen may, upon the advice of the Prime Minister, dissolve Parliament and proclaim a General Election. It is also possible that the Government may be defeated in the House of Commons on a major issue. It may then be forced to resign, in which case either the next strongest party forms a government, or a new election is sought. All but a handful of the Members of the House of Commons belong to one or other of the main political parties, and after a General Election it is the party with most Members which forms the Government. At certain times of national crisis, two or more parties may unite to form a Coalition Government.

New Laws start as Bills. Any Member of the Lords or Commons can introduce a Bill, though the majority are brought in by the Government, based on its plans as outlined in the Queen's Speech at the Opening of Parliament. The Bill has to pass through three Readings before it is considered to be agreed by the House of Commons. It then goes forward to the House of Lords. If it is a Financial Bill, the House of Lords must pass it without making any changes, but the Lords can reject any other Bill; after the lapse of a year, the Lords' rejection does not prevent its being passed and forwarded to the Queen for her Assent.

General Elections—Results

Party	Votes	Seats in the House of Commons
1970		
Conservative*	13,144,692	330
Labour	12,179,166	287
Liberal	2,177,638	6
Others	903,311	7

* *and associated parties*

54

1974 (Feb)

Labour	11,654,726	301
Conservative	11,963,207	296
Liberal	6,063,470	14
Others	1,651,823	24

1974 (Oct)

Labour	11,446,671	319
Conservatiue	10,445,951	276
Liberal	5,234,399	11
Communist	17,426	—
Plaid Cymru and Scottish Nationalist	982,172	13
Others	885,465	13

Awards and Rewards

Most countries reward their great men and women with decorations for gallantry in war, or titles for loyal and useful service in times of peace. In Britain, for example, a brilliant discovery by a scientist may gain him a knighthood or baronetcy.

The greatest international awards are the Nobel Prizes. Dr Alfred Nobel, the Swedish scientist who invented dynamite, left well over a million pounds to provide a fund which would award annual prizes of nearly £ 14,000 to the most deserving man or woman working in each of the following activities: Physics Research, Chemistry Research, Physiology and Medicine, Literature, Promotion of Peace.

In Britain, outstanding service may be rewarded by the creation of a peerage. No hereditary peerages have been created since 1965, but since 1958 many life peerages have

Victoria Cross

George Cross

Distinguished Service Order

Distinguished Conduct Medal

Distinguished Service Cross

George Medal

Military Cross

Air Force Cross

Distinguished Flying Cross

Distinguished Flying Medal

Air Force Medal

Albert Medal

Military Medal

Queen's Police Medal

 Red   Blue   Purple   Claret

56

been conferred. Other notable awards are the Orders of Chivalry, many of which confer a knighthood on the recipients. A special distinction for eminent men and women which does not confer a knighthood upon them is the Order of Merit, which is limited to 24 members, excluding foreign honorary members.

British Awards for Gallantry

The Victoria Cross. This was first awarded in June, 1856, and the bronze crosses were made from guns captured from the enemy during the Crimean War. The last of this metal was used up in 1942, and since then the crosses have been made of gun-metal from the Royal Mint. The cross is worn before all other decorations. It is one-and-a-half inches across, and bears the Royal Crown surmounted by a lion. It carries the inscription 'For Valour', and has a claret ribbon. The cross is awarded to anybody serving with or under the command of the armed forces, who performs an act of great bravery in the presence of the enemy.

The George Cross. First awarded in 1940, this decoration is a silver cross with a dark blue ribbon. The inscription is 'For Gallantry', and the design shows St George and the Dragon. It is awarded to civilians, and it is only given to members of the fighting services for the greatest gallantry in circumstances in which military awards could not normally be granted.

The Distinguished Service Order is awarded to officers of the armed services or the Merchant Navy.

The Distinguished Service Cross is for Royal Naval officers below the rank of captain, and warrant officers.

The Military Cross is awarded to captains, lieutenants and warrant officers in the Army and Indian and Colonial forces.

The Distinguished Flying Cross is for Royal Air Force and Fleet Air Arm officers and warrant officers for gallantry while flying in operations against the enemy.

Continued on page 60

British Military Insignia

NAVY	ARMY	R.A.F.
Admiral of the Fleet	Field Marshal	Marshal of the R.A.F.
Admiral	General	Air Chief Marshal
Vice-Admiral	Lieutenant-General	Air Marshal
Rear-Admiral	Major-General	Air Vice-Marshal
Commodore 2nd Class R.N	Brigadier	Air Commodore
Captain R.N.	Colonel	Group Captain
Commander R.N.	Lieutenant-Colonel	Wing Commander
Lieutenant-Commander R.N.	Major	Squadron Leader

58

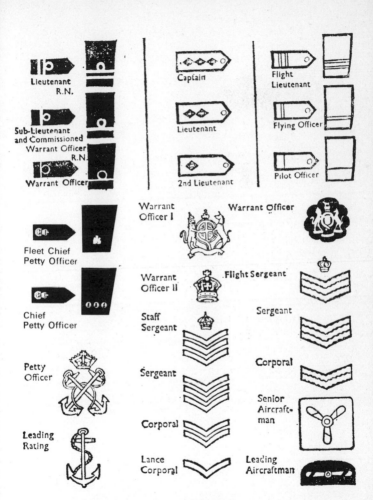

Lieutenant R.N.

Sub-Lieutenant and Commissioned Warrant Officer R.N.

Warrant Officer

Fleet Chief Petty Officer

Chief Petty Officer

Petty Officer

Leading Rating

Captain

Lieutenant

2nd Lieutenant

Warrant Officer I

Warrant Officer II

Staff Sergeant

Sergeant

Corporal

Lance Corporal

Flight Lieutenant

Flying Officer

Pilot Officer

Warrant Officer

Flight Sergeant

Sergeant

Corporal

Senior Aircraftman

Leading Aircraftman

The *Air Force Cross* is for acts of gallantry in the air but not in operations against the enemy.

The *Albert Medal* is given for gallantry in saving life at sea or on land.

The *Distinguished Conduct Medal* is awarded to warrant officers, non-commissioned officers and men of the Army and Royal Air Force.

The *Conspicuous Gallantry Medal* is for warrant officers and men of the Royal Navy, Merchant Navy or Royal Air Force.

The *George Medal* is given for acts of gallantry.

The *Edward Medal* is for heroic acts by miners or quarrymen, or by those engaged in rescuing them.

The *Distinguished Service Medal* is for chief petty officers, petty officers and men of the Royal Navy, and equivalent ranks in the Royal Marines and Merchant Navy.

The *Military Medal* is awarded to warrant officers, non-commissioned officers and men and women of the Army.

The *Distinguished Flying Medal* is awarded for gallantry to non-commissioned officers and men of the Royal Air Force while flying in operations against the enemy.

The Duke of Edinburgh's Award

This is a scheme begun in 1956 for young people between the ages of fifteen and eighteen, to encourage development of character. There are three awards—bronze, silver and gold—for attaining certain standards over a wide range of activities. To gain an award a boy must demonstrate his ability in self-reliance by planning and carrying out cross-country journeys, his fitness by reaching certain athletic standards, his competence in carrying out first aid and camp work, and his progress in his own chosen hobby. Boys intending to take part can obtain details through their schools or youth clubs.

PEOPLE AND
THE NEW WORLD

Early American Settlements

It was in the fifteenth century that the people of Europe began to look for new lands in which they could find broader commercial scope and, later, personal freedom. The American continent had been discovered by Scandinavian seamen five centuries earlier, but no settlements had remained. Voyagers such as Christopher Columbus believed that a westward course would lead them to India, and so when they reached America they called it the Indies.

Settlement in North, South and Central America was rapid. The Spanish and Portuguese colonised the South, the French and English the North. The struggles for power lasted for more than a century before the present boundaries and governments became settled. Britain at one time controlled all of eastern North America, but this direct government from London came to an end with the establishment of the United States as an independent nation during the War of 1775-1783 and the creation of Canada as a Dominion in 1867.

The development of the New World has been man's greatest achievement, for it required a mass migration of people, over a long period, from Europe and Africa to colonise such an enormous area as North America, which had previously been inhabited only by wandering indigenous tribes, wrongly called 'Indians'. Two hundred years ago the United States was a group of British colonies on the Eastern seaboard, still struggling to win a living from a new country, to cut back the forests and plough the land in

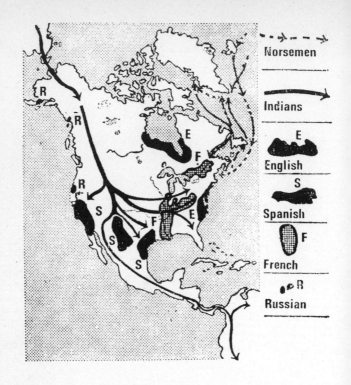

Norsemen

Indians

E
English

S
Spanish

F
French

R
Russian

order to grow crops which would pay for their imports from
Europe. Today the United States is the wealthiest nation in
the world, with one of the highest standards of living. In
material assets, it has more cars, telephones, television sets,
radios, etc., per thousand of its population than any other
nation. Canada, though slower to develop, has raised its
standard of living in very much the same way.

Canada

Canada is made up of twelve provinces and territories listed below with their dates of admission as provinces:

Province or Territory	Capital	Date of Admission	Population
Alberta	Edmonton	1905	1,627,874
British Columbia	Victoria	1871	2,184,621
Manitoba	Winnipeg	1870	922,000
New Brunswick	Fredericton	1867	634,577
Newfoundland	St. John's	1949	522,104
Nova Scotia	Halifax	1867	794,000
Ontario	Toronto	1867	7,703,106
Prince Edward Island	Charlottetown	1873	111,641
Quebec	Quebec	1867	6,027,764
Saskatchewan	Regina	1905	926,242
North-West Territories	Ottawa	—	34,807
Yukon Territory	Whitehorse	—	18,388

Ottawa is also the capital of all of Canada.

The United States

The United States is made up of fifty States and the Federal District of Columbia (Washington, D.C.). These are:

Name and Abbreviation	Capital	Date of Admission to the Union
Alabama (Ala.)	Montgomery	1819
Alaska	Juneau	1959
Arizona (Ariz.)	Phoenix	1912
Arkansas (Ark.)	Little Rock	1836
California (Calif.)	Sacramento	1850

Colorado (Colo.)	Denver	1876
Connecticut (Conn.)	Hartford	1788*
Delaware (Del.)	Dover	1787*
District of Columbia (D.C.)	Washington	1791
Florida (Fla.)	Tallahassee	1845
Georgia (Ga.)	Atlanta	1788*
Hawaii	Honolulu	1959
Idaho	Boise	1890
Illinois (Ill.)	Springfield	1818
Indiana (Ind.)	Indianopolis	1816
Iowa (Ia.)	Des Moines	1846
Kansas (Kans.)	Topeka	1861
Kentucky (Ky.)	Frankfort	1792
Louisiana (La.)	Baton Rouge	1812
Maine (Me.)	Augusta	1820
Maryland (Md.)	Annapolis	1788*
Massachusetts (Mass.)	Boston	1788*
Michigan (Mich.)	Lansing	1837
Minnesota (Minn.)	St. Paul	1858
Mississippi (Miss.)	Jackson	1817
Missouri (Mo.)	Jefferson City	1821
Montana (Mont.)	Helena	1889
Nebraska (Nebr.)	Lincoln	1867
Nevada (Nev.)	Carson City	1864
New Hampshire (N.H.)	Concord	1788*
New Jersey (N.J.)	Trenton	1787*
New Mexico (N. Mex.)	Santa Fé	1912
New York (N.Y.)	Albany	1788*
North Carolina (N.C.)	Raleigh	1789*
North Dakota (N. Dak.)	Bismarck	1889
Ohio	Columbus	1803
Oklahoma (Okla.)	Oklahoma City	1907
Oregon (Oreg.)	Salem	1859
Pennsylvania (Pa.)	Harrisburg	1787*
Rhode Island (R.I.)	Providence	1790*
South Carolina (S.C.)	Columbia	1788*

South Dakota (S. Dak.)	Pierre	1889
Tennessee (Tenn.)	Nashville	1796
Texas (Tex.)	Austin	1845
Utah	Salt Lake City	1896
Vermont (Vt.)	Montpelier	1791
Virginia (Va.)	Richmond	1788*
Washington (Wash.)	Olympia	1889
West Virginia (W.Va.)	Charleston	1863
Wisconsin (Wis.)	Madison	1848
Wyoming (Wyo.)	Cheyenne	1890

One of the Thirteen Original States

Growth of the United States in Population

= 5 million people

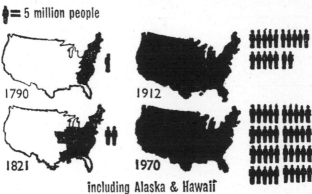

1790   1912

1821   1970

including Alaska & Hawaii

Presidents of the United States

In the American system of government the President combines his Presidential powers with many of those held by a Prime Minister under a system such as that in most Commonwealth countries, and is, therefore, a man of great

personal influence during his term of office. The Presidents
of the United States have been as follows

George Washington	Federalist		1789
John Adams	Federalist		1797
Thomas Jefferson	Republican		1801
James Madison	Republican		1809
James Monroe	Republican		1817
John Quincy Adams	Republican		1825
Andrew Jackson	Democratic		1829
Martin Van Buren	Democratic		1837
William Henry Harrison	Whig		1841
John Tyler	Whig		1841
James Knox Polk	Democratic		1845
Zachary Taylor	Whig		1849
Millard Fillmore	Whig		1850
Franklin Pierce	Democratic		1853
James Buchanan	Democratic		1857
Abraham Lincoln	Republican		1861
Andrew Johnson	Republican		1865
Ulysses Simpson Grant	Republican		1869
Rutherford Birchard Hayes	Republican		1877
James Abram Garfield	Republican		1881
Chester Alan Arthur	Republican		1881
Grover Cleveland	Democratic	1885 and	1893
Benjamin Harrison	Republican		1889
William McKinley	Republican		1897
Theodore Roosevelt	Republican		1901
William Howard Taft	Republican		1909
Woodrow Wilson	Democratic		1913
Warren Gamaliel Harding	Republican		1921
Calvin Coolidge	Republican		1923
Herbert Clark Hoover	Republican		1929
Franklin Delano Roosevelt	Democratic		1933
Harry S. Truman	Democratic		1945
Dwight D. Eisenhower	Republican		1953
John Fitzgerald Kennedy	Democratic		1961

Lyndon B. Johnson	Democratic	1963
Richard M. Nixon	Republican	1969
Gerald R. Ford	Republican	1974
James E. Carter	Democratic	1977

Central and South America and the Caribbean

The countries of Central and South America are independent, with the exception of French Guiana and Surinam (Netherlands Guiana), and a number of island dependencies. They are: —

Name	Date of Gaining Independence
Argentina	1816
Bolivia	1825
Brazil	1822
Chile	1818
Colombia	1819
Costa Rica	1821
Cuba	1902
Dominican Republic	1821
Ecuador	1822
Guatemala	1821
Guyana*	1966
Haiti	1804
Honduras	1821
Jamaica*	1962
Mexico	1810
Nicaragua	1821
Panama	1903
Paraguay	1811
Peru	1821
(El) Salvador	1821
Trinidad and Tobago*	1962
Uruguay	1825
Venezuela	1821

* *Member of the British Commonwealth of Nations*

67

PEOPLE ON THE MOVE

Two hundred years ago man's fastest way of travelling or sending a message was by horseback. The following information shows how much the picture has changed.

Man's Fastest Speed

The highest speed every travelled by man was achieved, not surprisingly, by astronauts. The Command Module of Apollo 10 carrying T. P. Stafford, E. A. Cernan and J. W. Young reached 24,791 m.p.h. (39,897 km per hour) on 26 May 1969.

Land Speed Record

The highest speed achieved on land was 627.287 m.p.h. (1,009 km per hour) by Gary Gabelich in 'The Blue Flame' on Bonneville Salt Flats, Utah, U.S.A. on 23 October 1970. During the run the natural gas-powered four-wheeled car was said to reach 650 m.p.h. (1,046 km per hour).

Water Speed Record

The record of 328 m.p.h., (528 km per hour) set up on Coniston Water in Lancashire in January, 1967, stands to the credit of the late Donald Campbell, who was the son of Sir Malcolm Campbell, holder of both land and water speed records in the nineteen-thirties.

Great Ships; The Blue Riband of the Atlantic

The fifteenth-century voyages of Columbus to America took many weeks of hardship; today it takes five days to cross from Britain to the United States and would take less than four days at maximum speeds. For nearly a century there has been keen competition between the great seafaring nations for the Blue Riband—the Championship of the Atlantic. The following table shows the progress of the Blue Riband since 1900.

Year	Direction	Ship	Tonnage	Time d.	h.	m.
1903	West-East	Deutschland (German)	16,502	5	4	48
1904	West-East	Kaiser Wilhelm II (German)	19,361	5	8	16
1909	East-West	Lusitania (British)	31,550	4	11	42
1909	East-West	Mauretania (British)	30,696	4	10	41
1929	West-East	Bremen (German)	51,650	4	14	30
1929	East-West	Bremen		4	18	17
1930	East-West	Europa (German)	51,656	4	17	6
1933	East-West	Bremen		4	17	43
1933	East-West	Rex (Italian)	50,000	4	13	58
1934	West-East	Empress of Britain (British)	42,348	4	6	58
1935	East-West	Normandie (French)	80,000	4	3	2
1936	East-West	Queen Mary (British)	81,237	4	0	27
1936	West-East	Queen Mary		3	23	57
1937	East-West	Normandie		3	23	2
1938	East-West	Queen Mary		3	21	45
1938	West-East	Queen Mary		3	20	42
1952	West-East	United States (American)	51,500	3	10	40
1952	East-West	United States		3	12	12

The largest ocean liners in the world are the FRANCE (French: 66,348 tons), QUEEN ELIZABETH 2 (British: 65,863 tons), RAFFAELLO (Italian: 45,933 tons), MICHEL-ANGELO (Italian: 45,911 tons), CANBERRA (British: 44,807 tons), ORIANA (British: 41,910 tons), UNITED STATES (U.S.A.: 38,216 tons), ROTTERDAM (Netherlands: 37,783 tons), NIEUW AMSTERDAM (Netherlands: 36,982 tons), and WINDSOR CASTLE (British: 36,123 tons). The largest ship afloat is GLOBTIK TOKYO (British: 238,252 tons).

Great Ship Canals

	Length		Width		Depth	
	(miles)	(km)	(feet)	(metres)	(feet)	(metres)
Gota (Sweden)	115	185	47	14	10	3
Suez (Egypt)	100	161	197	60	34	10.4
Kiel (Germany)	61	98	150	46	45	13.7
Panama (Panama)	50.5	81	300	91	45	13.7
Elbe (Germany)	41	66	72	22	10	3
Manchester (England)	35.5	57	120	37	28–30	9
Welland (Canada)	26.75	43	200	61	25	7.6
Princess Juliana (Netherlands)	20	32	52	16	16	4.9
Amsterdam (Netherlands)	16.5	26.5	88	27	23	7
Corinth (Greece)	4	6.5	72	22	26.25	8

Railways

The first steam railway locomotive was tried out in 1804 at Merthyr Tydfil in Wales, but the first to be successful was the famous Puffing Billy, installed at Wylam Colliery near Newcastle-on-Tyne in 1813, and in use until 1872 when it was bought by the government to be kept as a museum piece. In 1825 the Stockton and Darlington Railway was opened for goods traffic using a locomotive supplied by George Stephenson. Stephenson was the successful winner four years later, with his locomotive Rocket, of a competition to choose the locomotive for the Liverpool and Manchester Railway. Stephenson's locomotive drew thirty passengers at up to twenty-nine miles an hour. Today there are probably nearly a million miles of railway in the world, and the French have a locomotive capable of speeds over 200 miles per hour (320 km).

British Rail

The following are a few interesting facts and figures about British Rail:—

Largest station area	Clapham Junction, 34½ acres (14 hectares)
Largest number of platforms	Waterloo 21
Largest platform	Manchester Victoria & Exchange, 2,194 feet (668 metres)
Highest track altitude	Druimuachdar, 1,484 feet (452 metres) above sea level
Lowest point of railway	Severn Tunnel, 144 feet (44 metres) below sea level
Longest straight stretch	Between Selby and Hull Yorks., 18 miles (29 km)
Longest stretch of continuous four-track main line	St. Pancras to Glendon North Junction, Kettering, 74 miles 78 chains (120 km)
Longest bridge	Tay Bridge, 2 miles, 364 yards (3.55 km)
Longest tunnel	Severn Tunnel, 4 miles 628 yards (7.05 km)

The five Regions of British Rail are:

London Midland Region (formerly the London Midland and Scottish Company in the areas of England and Wales)
Western Region (formerly the Great Western Railway)
Southern Region (formerly the Southern Railway)
Eastern Region (formerly the Southern and North Eastern areas of the London and North Eastern Railway)
Scottish Region (formerly the Scottish areas of the London Midland and Scottish and the London and North Eastern Railways).

Great Railway Tunnels

Name	Location	Length Miles	(km)
London Transport (Northern Line, City Branch)	London	$17\frac{1}{3}$	28
Simplon	Switzerland — Italy	$12\frac{1}{4}$	20
Apennine	Italy	$11\frac{1}{2}$	18
St. Gotthard	Switzerland	$9\frac{1}{4}$	15
Lötschberg	Switzerland	9	$14\frac{1}{2}$
Mont Cenis	France — Italy	$8\frac{1}{2}$	13
Cascade	U.S.A.	$7\frac{3}{4}$	$12\frac{1}{4}$
Arlberg	Austria	$6\frac{1}{3}$	10
Moffat	U.S.A.	6	$9\frac{3}{4}$
Shimizu	Japan	6	$9\frac{3}{4}$
Kvineshei	Norway	$5\frac{3}{4}$	$9\frac{1}{4}$
Rimutaka	New Zealand	$5\frac{1}{2}$	$8\frac{3}{4}$
Otira	New Zealand	$5\frac{1}{4}$	$8\frac{1}{2}$
Tauern	Austria	$5\frac{1}{4}$	$8\frac{1}{2}$
Connaught	Canada	5	8
Ste. Marie-aux-Mines	France	$4\frac{1}{2}$	$7\frac{1}{4}$
Severn	England	$4\frac{1}{3}$	7

Principal Railway Gauges of the World

Gauge	Where in Use
5 ft 6 in. (1,676 mm)	Spain, Portugal, Argentina, Chile, India, Sri Lanka, Pakistan
5 ft 3 in. (1,600 mm)	Ireland, Brazil, Victoria (Australia), South Australia
5 ft 0 in. (1,524 mm)	U.S.S.R.
4 ft $8\frac{1}{2}$ in. (1,435 mm)	Great Britain, Europe (except Portugal, Spain, U.S.S.R.), Canada, U.S.A., Mexico, Uruguay, Peru, North

	Africa, Middle East, Egypt, Turkey, Australian Commonwealth, New South Wales (Australia), China, Korea
3 ft 6 in. (1,067 mm)	South and Western Australia, Queensland (Australia), New Zealand, Tasmania, South Africa, East and West Africa, Indonesia, Sudan, Sweden, Norway, Japan, Newfoundland (Canada), Costa Rica, Nicaragua, Honduras
3 ft 5¼ in. (1,048 mm)	Algeria, Jordan, Syria
3 ft 3⅜ in. (1,000 mm)	South America, East and West Africa, Malaysia, Burma, Thailand, Indo-China, Indonesia
3 ft 0 in. (914 mm)	Ireland, South America, El Salvador, Guatemala, Panama
2 ft 11 in. (889 mm)	Sweden
2 ft 6 in. (762 mm)	India, Ceylon
2 ft 0 in. (610 mm)	South America, India, Pakistan, Wales

Navigation

How does a ship find its way across thousands of miles of ocean and yet arrive at the harbour mouth as unerringly as a car steered home to its garage?

A nautical chart looks much like a road map, except that the roads are 'sea lanes', with lightships, buoys, shoals and sandbanks instead of towns, railways, church towers and hilltops. And, of course, the lines of latitude and longitude are clearly marked.

Before leaving port, the ship's navigator marks out his route on the chart. This chart is generally on what is known as 'Mercator's Projection', which means all the lines of longitude, or meridians, run parallel, whereas in reality, of course, they meet at the Poles. The compass points to *Magnetic* North, which is a variable number of miles away from *True* North, so that in working out the course the navigator must allow for this variation. This may be ten or more degrees—and it is found on the 'compass rose', a compass diagram printed on the chart at frequent intervals, or published in nautical tables.

For a course due East—90°—with a variation of 10° East the *Magnetic* course would be 80°. But before setting this for the helmsman, the navigator checks his deviation card—a note of any errors in the compass when it was last tested. Suppose the deviation is 2° West, then that would have to be *added* to the figure of 80° to give the final compass course that the helmsman will follow.

But the helm alone won't keep a ship on its course, so at sea the navigator uses the chronometer and sextant to check at regular intervals. The time of the ship's clocks is changed as it travels East or West of the Greenwich Meridian (0° longitude), and the difference between the ship's clocks (showing local time) and the chronometer (showing Greenwich time) tells the navigator his longitude. This is a simple calculation: there are 360° of longitude, and the earth turns once on its axis in every 24 hours; 360 divided by 24 gives us 15—which means one hour of 'sun's progress' equals 15°. When it is noon at Greenwich, it is 1 p.m. if you are 15° East, and 11 a.m. if you are 15° West.

Latitude is checked by a sextant. This is a device for measuring angles, and as we know from generations of navigation just where the sun ought to be at a given latitude on any particular occasion, and where each of the principal stars should appear at night, a check of the angle between the sun, moon or stars and the horizon provides a figure which need only be looked up in a standard book of tables carried by every ship.

This, of course, is the method out at sea, where no land-

74

marks are available to help in navigation. Along the coast the task of the officer on the bridge is much easier, for he can take bearings of lighthouses, church spires, prominent hilltops and other easily recognisable points marked on his chart. Where the bearings intersect is the ship's position.

Radio is another important aid to the navigator. He can take bearings from radio beacons—fixed points which send out radio signals in the same way that a lighthouse transmits intermittent beams of light. And, most important of all, he can use radar, a British invention which makes it possible for the navigator to know where ships, wrecks, buoys and other objects are in relation to his own vessel. The radar set sends out ultra-short-wave impulses in all directions; any of these striking an object sends back an echo to the set, and this appears as a bright dot on the monitor screen.

Distances by Sea

Using normal shipping routes, these are the distances of some of the world's principal seaports from Britain.

Name	Distance (miles)	(km)	Name	Distance (miles)	(km)
Alexandria	2,950	4,748	Mombasa	5,980	9,624
Basra	6,053	9,741	Montreal	2,760	4,448
Bombay	5,910	9,511	New York	3,118	5,018
Cape Town	5,978	9,620	Rangoon	7,590	12,215
Copenhagen	683	1,099	Rio de Janeiro	5,030	8,095
Gothenburg	584	940	Sydney	12,201	19,636
Hong Kong	9,743	15,680	Tunis	2,050	3,298
Karachi	5,730	9,221	Valparaiso	7,207	11,598
Manila	9,650	15,530	Wellington	11,096	17,857
Marseilles	1,833	2,950	Yokohama	11,536	18,565

Notable Bridges of the World

The world's longest bridge spans by type are as follows:

Suspension: Verrazano-Narrows Bridge, New York, built 1964. Length: 4,260 feet (1,298 metres).
Cantilever: Quebec Railway Bridge, Quebec, built 1917. Length: 1,800 feet (549 metres).
Steel Arch: Bayonne Bridge, New York, built 1931. Length: 1,652 feet (504 metres).
Covered Bridge: Hartland, New Brunswick. Length: 1,282 feet (391 metres).
Concrete Arch: Gladesville, Sydney, built 1964. Length: 1,000 feet (305 metres).
Stone Arch: Plauen, East Germany, built 1903. Length: 295 feet (90 metres).

The longest bridge span in Great Britain is the Firth of Forth road bridge, built in 1964, which has a main span of 3,300 feet (1,006 metres).

The world's longest railway bridge (built 1935) is the Huey P. Long Bridge in Louisiana, which carries the railway 4.35 miles (7 km). Its longest span is 790 feet (240 metres).

The world's highest bridge (built 1929) is over the Arkansas River in Colorado, and is 1,053 feet (321 metres) above the water level. The world's longest viaduct (road-carrying bridge) is the Second Lake Ponchartrain Causeway (built 1969) in Louisiana and is 23.87 miles (38.42 km) long.

The world's longest aqueduct (water-carrying bridge) is the California Aqueduct (built 1974) which is 444 miles (715 km) long. The longest aqueduct in Great Britain is the Pontcysyllte Aqueduct carrying the Shropshire Union Canal over the River Dee. Built in 1803 it is 1,007 feet (306 metres) long and 121 feet (37 metres) high.

Distances by Air

These are the distances of principal world cities from London by air, using the shortest routes.

Name	Distance (miles)	(km)	Name	Distance (miles)	(km)
Aden	4,104	6,604	Melbourne	11,934	19,206
Amsterdam	231	372	Montreal	3,310	5,327
Athens	1,501	2,416	Moscow	1,549	2,493
Baghdad	3,063	4,929	Munich	588	946
Berlin	593	954	Nairobi	4,429	7,128
Bombay	4,901	7,887	New York	3,500	5,633
Brussels	218	351	Nicosia	2,028	3,264
Chicago	4,127	6,641	Oslo	722	1,162
Colombo	5,854	9,421	Paris	215	346
Copenhagen	609	980	Prague	670	1,078
Diakarta	8,337	13,417	Rome	908	1,461
Geneva	468	753	San Francisco	6,169	9,928
Gibraltar	1,085	1,746	Singapore	7,678	12,357
Hong-Kong	8,102	13,038	Stockholm	899	1,447
Johannesburg	6,227	10,021	Teheran	3,419	5,502
Karachi	4,428	7,126	Tel Aviv	2,230	3,589
Kingston	5,207	8,379	Tokyo	10,066	16,200
Kuala Lumpur	7,883	12,686	Venice	703	1,131
Lagos	3,401	5,473	Vienna	791	1,273
Lisbon	972	1,565	Warsaw	914	1,471
Madrid	775	1,247			

Local Time Throughout the World

As you travel eastwards from Greenwich, the longitude time (see under **Navigation**) is one hour later for every 15°; to the west it is an hour earlier. But for convenience local clocks don't always show the correct longitude time, otherwise travellers inside even a quite small country would be constantly confused. In Britain, all clocks show Greenwich

Mean Time except when Summer Time is in operation. Only in large countries such as Canada, the U.S.S.R., the United States, etc., are time zones necessary.

Summer Time in the United Kingdom is one hour in advance of G.M.T. Many other countries of the world have annual variations from standard time, usually known as Summer Time or Daylight Saving Time. It should be remembered when using the following table, therefore, that there are seasonal variations, and indeed that in the summer local time in Great Britain is 1 p.m. at noon G.M.T.

Here are the local times in various big cities when it is noon (G.M.T.) in London:

City	Time	City	Time
Adelaide		Cape Town	
(Australia)	9.30 p.m.	(South Africa)	2 p.m.
Algiers	1 p.m.	Caracas	
Amsterdam		(Venezuela)	8 a.m.
(Netherlands)	1 p.m.	Chicago (U.S.A.)	6 a.m.
Ankara (Turkey)	2 p.m.	Colombo	
Athens (Greece)	2 p.m.	(Sri Lanka)	5.30 p.m.
Belgrade		Copenhagen	
(Yugoslavia)	1 p.m.	(Denmark)	1 p.m.
Berlin (Germany)	1 p.m.	Djakarta	
Bombay (India)	5.30 p.m.	(Indonesia)	8 p.m.
Boston (U.S.A.)	7 a.m.	Edinburgh	
Brussels (Belgium)	1 p.m.	(Scotland)	noon
Bucharest		Gibraltar	1 p.m.
(Romania)	2 p.m.	Guatemala City	
Budapest		(Guatemala)	6 a.m.
(Hungary)	1 p.m.	Guayaquil	
Buenos Aires		(Ecuador)	7 a.m.
(Argentina)	9 a.m.	Halifax (Canada)	8 a.m.
Cairo (Egypt)	2 p.m.	Havana (Cuba)	7 a.m.
Calcutta (India)	5.30 p.m.	Helsinki (Finland)	2 p.m.
Canton (China)	8 p.m.	Hobart (Tasmania)	10 p.m.

Hong Kong	8 p.m.	Peking (China)	8 p.m.
Johannesburg		Perth (Australia)	8 p.m.
(South Africa)	2 p.m.	Prague	
Karachi		(Czechoslovakia)	1 p.m.
(Pakistan)	5 p.m.	Rangoon	
Kingston	7 a.m.	(Burma)	6.30 p.m.
(Jamaica)		Reykjavik	
La Paz (Bolivia)	8 a.m.	(Iceland)	noon
Leningrad		Rio de Janeiro	
(U.S.S.R.)	3 p.m.	(Brazil)	9 a.m.
Lima (Peru)	7 a.m.	Rome (Italy)	1 p.m.
Lisbon (Portugal)	1 p.m.	San Francisco	
Madrid (Spain)	1 p.m.	(U.S.A.)	4 a.m.
Manila (Philippine		Santiago (Chile)	8 a.m.
Islands)	8 p.m.	Shanghai (China)	8 p.m.
Mecca		Singapore	7.30 p.m.
(Saudi Arabia)	3 p.m.	Sofia (Bulgaria)	2 p.m.
Melbourne		Stockholm	
(Australia)	10 p.m.	(Sweden)	1 p.m.
Mexico City		Sydney	
(Mexico)	6 a.m.	(Australia)	10 p.m.
Montevideo		Teheran (Iran)	3.30 p.m.
(Uruguay)	9 a.m.	Tel Aviv (Israel)	2 p.m.
Montreal		Tokyo (Japan)	9 p.m.
(Canada)	7 a.m.	Toronto (Canada)	7 a.m.
Moscow		Vancouver	
(U.S.S.R.)	3 p.m.	(Canada)	4 a.m.
Nairobi (Kenya)	3 p.m.	Vienna (Austria)	1 p.m.
New Orleans		Warsaw (Poland)	1 p.m.
(U.S.A.)	6 a.m.	Wellington	
New York		(New Zealand)	midnight
(U.S.A.)	7 a.m.	Winnipeg	
Oslo (Norway)	1 p.m.	(Canada)	6 a.m.
Panama City		Zürich	
(Panama)	7 a.m.	(Switzerland)	1 p.m.
Paris (France)	1 p.m.		

Aircraft Spotting

When travelling by air you can easily tell the country of origin of other aircraft you see around you by their registration marks. All planes other than military aircraft carry two groups of letters on the wings. The first group indicates the country of origin, thus 'G-ABC' would be a British aircraft with the distinguishing letters 'ABC'. Many of the national markings are as follows:

Marking	Country	Marking	Country
AN	Nicaragua	HI	Dominican Republic
AP	Pakistan		
B	Formosa	HK	Colombia
CC	Chile	HL	Korea
CCCP	U.S.S.R.	HP	Panama
CF	Canada	HS	Thailand
CN	Morocco	HZ	Saudi Arabia
CP	Bolivia	I	Italy
CS	Portugal	JA	Japan
CU	Cuba	JY	Jordan
CX	Uruguay	LG	Guatemala
CZ	Monaco	LN	Norway
D	Germany	LV	Argentina
EC	Spain	LX	Luxembourg
EI	Ireland	LZ	Bulgaria
EL	Liberia	N	U.S.A.
EP	Iran	OB	Peru
ET	Ethiopia	OD	Lebanon
F	France	OE	Austria
G	Great Britain	OH	Finland
HA	Hungary	OK	Czechoslovakia
HB	Switzerland	OO	Belgium
HC	Ecuador	OY	Denmark
HH	Haiti	PH	Netherlands

PI	Philippine Islands	XA, XB, XC	Mexico
PJ	Netherlands Antilles	XH	Honduras
		XT	China
PK	Indonesia	XY, XZ	Burma
PP, PT	Brazil	YA	Afghanistan
PZ	Surinam	YE	Yemen
SA	Libya	YI	Iraq
SE	Sweden	YJ	New Hebrides
SN	Sudan	YK	Syria
SP	Poland	YR	Romania
SU	Egypt	YS	(El) Salvador
SX	Greece	YU	Yugoslavia
TC	Turkey	YV	Venezuela
TF	Iceland	ZA	Albania
TI	Costa Rica	ZK	New Zealand
VH	Australia	ZP	Paraguay
VQ, VP,	British Colonies	ZS	South Africa
VR	and British Protectorates	3W	Vietnam
		4R	Sri Lanka
VT	India	4X	Israel

Car Spotting

If you're keen on car spotting, carry your Handbook with you when you're on a journey. The following tables will help you to identify cars from overseas, for cars travelling outside their countries of registration carry special identification letters as well as their normal registration plates. The national markings are:

Marking	**Country**	**Marking**	**Country**
A	Austria	AUS	Australia,* Norfolk Islands*
ADN	Aden State*		
AL	Albania		
AND	Andorra	B	Belgium

81

BDS	Barbados*		nea and Spanish Sahara
BG	Bulgaria		
BH	Belize*	EAK	Kenya*
BL	Lesotho*	EAT	Tanzania*
BP	Botswana*	EAU	Uganda*
BR	Brazil	EAZ	Tanzania*
BRG	Guyana*	EC	Ecuador
BRN	Bahrain*	ET	Egypt
BRU	Brunei*	F	France, and
BS	Bahamas*		French
BUR	Burma*		Overseas
C	Cuba		departments
CDN	Canada	FL	Liechtenstein
CGO	Congo	GB	Great Britain
	(Leopoldville)		and Northern
CH	Switzerland		Ireland*
CI	Ivory Coast	GBA	Alderney*
CL	Sri Lanka	GBG	Guernsey*
CNB	Malaysia*	GBJ	Jersey*
CO	Colombia	GBM	Isle of Man*
CR	Costa Rica	GBY	Malta,* Gozo*
CS	Czechoslovakia	GBZ	Gibraltar
CY	Cyprus*	GCA	Guatemala
D	Germany	GH	Ghana*
	(Federal	GR	Greece, Crete,
	Republic)		Dodecanese
DK	Denmark,		Islands
	Faroe Islands	H	Hungary
DOM	Dominican	HK	Hong Kong*
	Republic	I	Italy, Sardinia,
DY	Dahomey		Sicily
DZ	Algeria	IL	Israel
E	Spain, Balearic	IND	India*
	Islands, Ca-	IR	Iran
	nary Islands,	IRL	Republic of
	Spanish Gui-		Ireland (Eire)*

IRQ	Iraq	(Angola), São
IS	Iceland*	João Baptista
J	Japan*	de Ajuda,
JA	Jamaica,*	St Thomé
	Cayman	and Principé
	Islands,*	Islands
	Turks and	PA	Panama
	Caicos Islands*	PAK	Pakistan*
JOR	Jordan	PE	Peru
K	Cambodia	PI	Philippine
KWT	Kuwait		Islands
L	Luxembourg	PL	Poland
LAO	Laos	PTM	Malaysia*
LT	Libya	PY	Paraguay
MA	Morocco	R	Romania
MC	Monaco	RA	Argentina
MEX	Mexico	RCA	Central African
MS	Mauritius*		Republic
N	Norway	RCB	Zaire
NA	Netherlands	RCH	Chile
	Antilles	RH	Haiti
NGN	West Irian	RI	Indonesia
NIC	Nicaragua	RIM	Islamic Republic
NIG	Niger*		of Mauretania
NL	Netherlands	RL	Lebanon
	(Holland)	RM	Malagasy
NZ	New Zealand*		Republic
P	Portugal, The	RMM	Mali
	Azores, Cape	Z	Zambia*
	Verde Islands,	RNY	Malawi*
	Madeira,	RSM	San Marino
	Mozambique,	RSR	Rhodesia*
	Portuguese	RWA	Republic of
	Timor,		Ruanda and
	Portuguese		Kingdom
	West Africa		of Burundi

S	Sweden		of America
SA	Saar	V	Vatican City
SD	Swaziland*		State
SF	Finland	VN	Vietnam
SGP	Singapore*	WAG	Gambia*
SK	Sarawak*	WAL	Sierra Leone*
SME	Surinam	WAN	Nigeria*
SN	Republic	WD	Dominica
	of Senegal		(Windward
SU	Union of Soviet		Islands)*
	Socialist	WG	Grenada
	Republics		(Windward
SUD	Sudan		Islands)*
SWA	South West	WL	St. Lucia
	Africa		(Windward
SY	Seychelles*		Islands)*
SYR	Syria	WS	Western
T	Thailand*		Samoa*
TD	Trinidad and	WV	St. Vincent
	Tobago*		(Windward
TG	Togo		Islands)*
TN	Tunisia	YU	Yugoslavia
TR	Turkey	YV	Venezuela
TT	Togo	ZA	Republic
U	Uruguay		of South
USA	United States		Africa*

In countries marked with an asterisk, the rule of the road is Drive on the Left; otherwise Drive on the Right.

Signalling

Travel and communications require efficient systems of signalling. In 1588, when the Spanish Armada threatened to attack Britain, huge bonfires were built on hilltops across the

84

country, and it was arranged that if invasion came, these bonfires would be lit in turn to pass the warning. Later came signal stations on hilltops, relaying messages by means of mirrors reflecting the sun. These were in use by the Royal Navy for sending messages between London and Portsmouth Dockyard from 1795 until 1847. During the last thirty years before the electric telegraph replaced these signal stations, the system in use was the Semaphore Code, using a mast with two arms. Semaphore is now used mainly as a method of flag signalling by scouts, campers and mountaineers.

Semaphore Code

Before starting a Semaphore message it is customary to hoist the letters 'VOX' or 'I' in International Code flags. Transmission is opened by giving the Alphabetical Sign, then waiting for the signal 'C' in reply as an indication to go ahead. When numbers are to be sent, the Numerical Sign is made; on return to ordinary letters the Alphabetical Sign is given.

Ships at sea communicate by radio, Morse Code transmitted by signal lamps or Brown's International Code of flag signals. The flag signals are shown on the next page.

An abbreviated code of single letter signals, is used to transmit the following standard messages:

A : I have a diver down; keep well clear at slow speed.
B : I am taking in, or discharging, or carrying dangerous goods.
C : Yes.
D : Keep clear of me; I am manoeuvring with difficulty.
E : I am altering my course to starboard.
F : I am disabled; communicate with me.
G : I require a pilot.
H : I have a pilot on board.
I : I am altering my course.
J : I am on fire and have dangerous cargo on board; keep well clear of me.
K : I wish to communicate with you.
L : You should stop your vessel instantly.
M : My vessel is stopped and making no way through the water.
N : No.
O : Man overboard.
P : *In Harbour* — all persons should report on board as the vessel is about to proceed to sea.
At Sea — It may be used by fishing vessels to mean "My nets have come fast upon an obstruction."
Q : My vessel is 'healthy' and I request free pratique.
S : My engines are going astern.
T : Keep clear of me; I am engaged in pair trawling.
U : You are running into danger.
V : I require assistance.

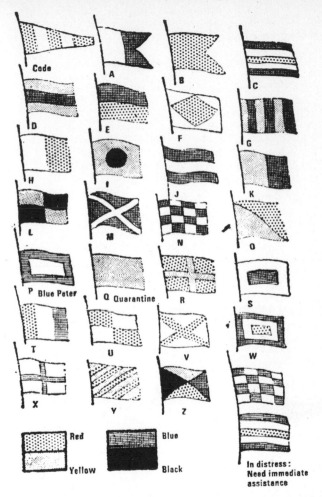

Code

A

B

C

D

E

F

G

H

I

J

K

L

M

N

O

P Blue Peter

Q Quarantine

R

S

T

U

V

W

X

Y

Z

Red

Yellow

Blue

Black

In distress:
Need immediate
assistance

W : I require medical assistance.
X : Stop carrying out your intentions and watch for my signals.
Y : I am dragging my anchor.
Z : I require a tug.

The following combinations of two letters on the halyards hoisted to the yardarm signify:

AD: I must abandon my ship.
IX: Fire is gaining.
KA: I urgently require a collision mat.
KT: You should send me a towing hawser.
NC: I am in distress and need immediate assistance.

Morse Code

An American artist, Samuel F. B. Morse (1791 — 1872), invented the Code that bears his name, to simplify the method of sending messages by telegraph—of which he has equal claim with Britain's Professor Wheatstone to be the inventor. Morse can be sent on a hand key by a skilled operator at up to twenty-five words a minute, but automatic transmitters can exceed this many times, and also 'scramble' the coded message by variations of speed so that only a receiving set equipped with the same system of speed controls can interpret it.

The Code consists of dots and dashes, a dash being equal to three dots. A gap equal to one dot is left between each symbol; twice as much is left between each letter, and a longer break, preferably at least the length of a dash, between words.

The International Morse code is as follows:

A .—
B —...
C —.—.
D —..
E .

F ..—.
G ——.
H ....
I ..
J .———

K	—.—	X	—..—
L	.—..	Y	—.——
M	——	Z	——..
N	—.	1	.————
O	———	2	..———
P	.——.	3	...——
Q	——.—	4	....—
R	.—.	5	.....
S	...	6	—....
T	—	7	——...
U	..—	8	———..
V	...—	9	————.
W	.——	0	—————

Full stop	.—.—.—
Semicolon	—.—.—.
Comma	——..——
Colon	———...
Interrogation	..——..
Apostrophe	.————.
Hyphen	—....—
Bracket	—.——.—
Inverted commas	.—..—.
Underline	..——.—
Double dash	—...—
Distress signal (S.O.S.)	...———...
Attention signal	—.—.—
Invitation to transmit	—.—
Wait	.—...
Break	—...—
Understood	...—.
Error	....
Received	.—.
Position report	—.—.
End of message	.—.—.
Finish of transmission	...—.—

PEOPLE AND LANGUAGE

The Development of the Alphabet. We do not know the point in man's development at which he first made sound which could be described as 'language'. The tracing of the history of written language, however, has been possible to a high degree of accuracy, and the diagram on the following page indicates how most of our present-day letters came to be formed.

Column I shows Egyptian hieroglyphics, or picture-writing, facing to the left. Column II is of later Egyptian writing, in which the picture has become unrecognisable, and the direction has changed to the right. Column III shows the progress made by the time of the Phoenicians and Column VI contains the fairly similar alphabet of early Greek civilisation. Columns V, VI and VII show further development by the Greeks; in Columns VIII, IX and X are the stages through which the Romans progressed, leaving as their legacy most of the present-day alphabet of the Western world.

The English Language

Our own language, English, is a mixture of words drawn from the vocabularies of the various invaders of Britain over a period of some two thousand years. That is why in English there are often several different words meaning roughly the same thing, some having Anglo-Saxon origins and others coming from Latin. Our language is also less 'regular' than French, Italian or Spanish, all of which have direct Latin origins.

Words are placed in categories according to how they are used. These categories are known as parts of speech. The English language has eight parts of speech. They are listed below.

Noun : the name of a person, place or thing. Nouns are of four Genders: Masculine, Feminine, Common and Neuter.

#	EGYPTIAN			GREEK				LATIN		
1	🦅	ح	△	A	A	ᴅ	ɑ	A	A	ɑɑɑ
2	🐫	ട	𝟿	ჳ	B	B	B	B	B	Bb
3	⌂	⋝	⁊	ᒋ	Γ	Γ	ΓΥ	ᑦ	C	cɢɢɢ
4	⌔	⊲	Δ	Δ	Δ	Δ̇	δ	▷	D	δδδ
5	⊓	Ⅲ	⍺	ᴈ	E	ᴇ	ᴇ	ᴇ	E	ee
6	✶	↵	५	५	ᐯF		F	F	F	Ff
7	🐍	ᒕ	‡	‡	I	Z	ᴢᴇ	‡	Z	z
8	🐚	○	⌱	⊟	H	H	hη	⊟	H	hh
9	⊂	⊃	⊕	⊕	⊙	Θ	ᘐ	⊕		
10	⑊	⅄	⌇	ᘓ	⏐	ɩ	ᒄ	⏐	⏐	ij
11	⊂	ᖰ	५	∓	K	K	ᴋᴋ	K	K	κ
12	ᗉ	ᒪ	ʟ	✓	⋀	⋋	⋌	ʟ	L	ll
13	🦉	ᴣ	ᴹ	ᴍ	Μ	Μ	ᴍᴍ	ᴍ	Μ	mm
14	〰	↵	५	ᴎ	Ν	Ν	ᴩᴦ	ᴦ	Ν	nn
15	↔	ᖡ	∓	∓	Ξ	ᴣ	ᴌ	⊞	†	xx
16		⌒	O	∘	O	O	∘	O		
17	▦	ᵭᴸ	⌐	⌐	Γ	π	πω	P	P	P
18	ᴖ	ᵴ	ᴦ	ᴎ	Μ		ᴌ	ᴦ		
19	Δ	⊿	φ	φ	ϙ			φ	Q	qq
20	⊖	ᴀ	ᴿ	ᴀ	P	P	ᴇᴘ	ᴚ	R	Rr
21	👑	ᴣ	W	ᴣ	ᴌ	C	ᴄσ	ᴣ	S	ſfs
22	ᶂ	ᴃ	†	T	T	T	ᴛ	T	T	tt

These Genders can be illustrated by the following words: man, woman, cousin, hat. Nouns are either Singular or Plural, examples of both being: dog and dogs, penny and pence. Classes of nouns are Proper (the name of a particular person, place or thing, e.g. William, France) and Common (the name common to everything in one group, e.g. house, car).

English nouns have three Cases which they take to show their relation to the rest of a sentence. These are Nominative (denoting the person or thing taking action), Objective (the person or thing about which action is taken) and Possessive (that which belongs to a person or thing).

Adjective: a word which describes or qualifies a noun. Adjectives may be divided into three categories: those which express Quality (*bad* company), those expressing Quantity (*ten* boys) and Demonstrative Adjectives (*that* window). There are three degrees of comparison in adjectives— Positive, Comparative and Superlative, examples of which are: good, better, best; young, younger, youngest.

The Articles (Definite: the; Indefinite: a, an) are also adjectives, as are the Numerals (Cardinal: one, two; Ordinal: first, second; Multiplicative: once, twice; Indefinite: many, few).

Pronoun: a word used in place of a noun. Pronouns, like nouns, have Gender, Number and Case. Pronouns may be Personal (I, she, you), Relative (that, who), Demonstrative (this, those), Indefinite (some, one), Interrogative (who? which?), Distributive (either, each) and Reflexive (yourself, themselves).

Verb: a word which states the action of a noun. Verbs are either Transitive or Intransitive. Transitive verbs describe an action which affects an object, e.g. 'I start the car'. Intransitive verbs do not affect an object, e.g. 'The car starts.' 'I start the car' is an example of a verb in Active Voice; in Passive Voice it would be 'The car was started by me.'

Verbs have three Finite Moods: Indicative (I speak); Imperative (Speak!); Subjunctive (I may speak). There is also the Infinitive Mood (to speak).

There are two Participles, used with such verbs as *to be* and *to have*: the Present Participle (speaking) and the Past Participle (spoken). There is also a verbal noun, the Gerund (the *speaking* of English).

The Tense of a verb shows the time of its action (Past, Present, Future). The degrees of completeness of the action are: Simple (I speak, I spoke, I shall speak); Continuous (I am speaking; I was speaking, I shall be speaking); Perfect (I have spoken, I had spoken, I shall have spoken); Perfect Continuous (I have been speaking, I had been speaking I shall have been speaking).

Adverb : a word which modifies or qualifies a verb, an adjective or another adverb. Adverbs can be divided into the following categories: Time (often, now); Place (here, outside); Quality (well, beautifully); Quantity (enough, almost); Number (once); Cause (therefore, why); Mood (perhaps).

Preposition : a word which shows the relation between words in a sentence. Examples of prepositions are: to, on, by, of, from, for, through, about, after, except, towards.

Conjunction : a word which links words, phrases, clauses or sentences. Examples of conjunctions are: and, but, for, because, also, unless, though, therefore.

Interjection : a word standing alone in a sentence, expressing strong emotion. Examples are: Indeed! Goodness! Bother! Oh! Alas!

Foreign Words and Phrases

There are many foreign expressions used in English, a number of which are quite convenient in that there is no exact equivalent in our language. Here are some in common use (Abbreviations—F: French; G: German; Gk: Greek; I: Italian; L: Latin; P: Portuguese; S: Spanish).

ad hoc (L). For this special object.

ad infinitum (L). For ever; to infinity.

ad interim (L). Meanwhile.

ad libitum (ad lib.) (L). To any extent; at pleasure.

ad nauseam (L). To the point of disgust.

adsum (L). I am here.

ad valorem (L). According to value.

affaire d'honneur (F). Affair of honour; duel.

a fortiori (L). With stronger reason.

à la bonne heure (F). Well done; that's good.

à la carte (F). From the full menu.

à la mode (F). In the fashion.

alter ego (L). Other self.

amour-propre (F). Self-esteem.

a posteriori (L). From the effect to the cause.

a priori (L). From the cause to the effect.

à propos (F). To the point.

arrière-pensée (F). Mental reservation.

au contraire (F). On the contrary.

au courant (F). Fully acquainted (with).

auf Wiedersehen (G). Till we meet again.

au naturel (F). In a natural state.

au pair (F). On an exchange basis.

au revoir (F). Till we meet again.

auto da fé (P). Act of faith.

à votre santé (F). Your good health!

bête noire (F). Pet hate.

billet doux (F). Love letter.

bona fide (L). In good faith; genuine.

bon marché (F). A bargain; cheap.

bon vivant (F). Gourmet; one who enjoys life.

bon voyage (F). Have a good journey.

canaille (F). Common mob (term of contempt).

carpe diem (L). Enjoy today.

carte blanche (F). Full powers.

casus belli (L). Cause of war.

caveat emport (L). Let the buyer beware.

chacun à son goût (F). Everyone to his own taste.

chef-d'œuvre (F). Masterpiece.

cherchez la femme (F). Look for the woman (in the case).

ci-devant (F). Former.

comme il faut (F). In good taste.

compos mentis (L). In full possession of sanity.

corps de ballet (F). The team of dancers in a ballet.

corps diplomatique (F). The group of diplomats in a capital city.

cui bono? (L). Who will get any benefit?

cum grano salis (L). With a grain of salt.

d'accord (F). Agreed.

de facto (L). In fact.

de jure (L). By right (in law).

de luxe (F). Of especially high quality.

de rigueur (F). Necessary.

dernier cri (F). The latest fashion.

de trop (F). Superfluous; not wanted.

deus ex machina (L). Providential interposition; nick-of-time solution by a superhuman agency.

Dieu et mon droit (F). God and my right (motto of the British Crown).

double entente (F). Double meaning (sometimes *double entendre*).

embarras de richesse (F). Difficulty caused by having too much.

en deshabillé (F). Dressed in clothes suitable only for lounging.

en famille (F). In the family; informal.

en fête (F). Clebrating.

en passant (F). In passing; by the way.

en rapport (F). In sympathy; in harmony.
entre nous (F). Between ourselves.
esprit de corps (F). Group spirit.
ex cathedra (L). From the chair of office, with authority.
ex libris (L). From the books (of).

fait accompli (F). An accomplished fact.
faux pas (F). False step; mistake.
femme de chambre (F). Chambermaid.
fête champêtre (F.) Gala occasion in the open air.
fiat lux (L). Let there be light.
fin de siècle (F). Decadent.

gitano (S). Gipsy.
gourmet (F). Lover of good food.

Hausfrau (G). Housewife.
hic jacet (L). Here lies.
hoi poliol (Gk). The people.
honi soit qui mal y pense (F). Shamed be he who thinks evil of it.
hors de combat (F). No longer able to fight.

ibidem (ibid.) (L). In the same place.
ich dien (G). I serve.
idée fixe (F). Obsession.
in extremis (L). At the point of death.
infra dignitatem (infra dig.) (L). Beneath one's dignity.
in loco parentis (L). In the place of a parent.
in memoriam (L). In memory (of).
in perpetuum (L). For ever.
in re (L). In the matter of.
in situ (L). In its original position.
inter alia (L). Among other things.
in toto (L). Completely.
ipso facto (L). (Obvious) from the facts.
ipso jure (L). By the law itself.

96

je ne sais quoi (F). I know not what.

jeu d'esprit (F). Witticism.

laissez faire (F). Leave matters alone: a policy of non-interference.

lares et penates (L). Household gods.

lèse-majesté (F). High treason or arrogant conduct of inferiors.

locum tenens (L). A substitute or deputy.

magnum opus (L). A great work; an author's principal book.

maitre d'hôtel (F). Hotel-keeper; head waiter.

mal de mer (F). Sea-sickness.

mañana (S). Tomorrow (will do as well as today).

mariage de convenance (F). A marriage arranged for money or other material considerations.

mea culpa (L). It is my fault.

modus operandi (L). Method of working.

multum in parvo (L). Much in little.

mutatis mutandis (L). The necessary changes having been made.

non plus ultra (L). Nothing further; the summit of achievement.

nil desperandum (L). Despair of nothing.

noblesse oblige (F). Noble birth imposes obligations.

nom de guerre (F). Assumed name.

nom de plume (F). Assumed name of an author.

non compos mentis (L). Of unsound mind.

non sequitur (L). It does not follow.

nota bene (N. B.) (L). Note well.

nouveau riche (F). Newly rich.

opus (L). Work (of art, music or literature).

outré (F). Eccentric; outside the bounds of propriety.

pace (L). By leave of.
par excellence (F). Pre-eminently.
par exemple (F). For example.
passim (L). Everywhere.
pax vobiscum (L). Peace be with you.
per annum (L). By the year.
per capita (L). By the head.
per centum (per cent) (L). By the hundred.
per diem (L). By the day.
per mensem (L). By the month.
persona grata (L). An acceptable person.
persona non grata.(L). An unacceptable person.
pièce de résistance (F). Chief dish of meal; main item.
pied-à-terre (F). Lodging for occasional visits.
poste restante (F). To await collection (from a post office).
prima ballerina (I). Principal female dancer in a ballet.
prima donna (I). Principal female singer in an opera.
prima facie (L). At first sight.
pro forma (L). As a matter of form.
pro rata (L). In proportion.
prosit (G). Good health!
pro tempore (L). For the time being.

quid pro quo (L). Something offered for another of the same value.
quien sabe? (S). Who knows?
quo vadis (L). Whither thou goest?

raison d'être (F). Reason for existence.
rara avis (L). A rare bird; unusual person or thing.
reduction ad absurdum (L). A reducing to the absurd.
rendez-vous (F). Meeting-place.
requiescat in pace (R. I. P.) (L). Rest in peace.
résumé (F). Summary.

sans souçi (F). Without care.
sauve qui peut (F). Save himself who can.
savoir-faire (F). Tact.
semper fidelis (L). Always faithful.
sine die (L). Indefinitely.
sine qua non (L). An indispensable condition.
sobriquet (F). Nickname.
soi-disant (F). Self-styled.
sotto voce (I). In a whisper or undertone.
status quo (L). The existing state of affairs.
stet (L). Let it stand (ignore correction marks).
sub judice (L). Before a judge (and not yet decided).
sub rosa (L). Under the rose; secretly.
sui generis (L). Of its own kind; unique.

table d'hôte (F). A set meal at a fixed price.
tempus fugit (L). Time flies.
terra firma (L). Solid earth.
tête-à-tête (F). Private talk between two people.
tour de force (F). Feat of skill or strength.
tout de suite (F). Immediately.
tout ensemble (F). Taken all together.

ubique (L). Everywhere.
ultima Thule (L). The utmost boundary.

vade mecum (L). A constant companion; a manual of reference.
versus (L). Against.
vice versa (L). Conversely.
vis-à-vis (F). Opposite; face to face.

wagon-lit (F). Railway sleeping-car.
Weltschmerz (G). World weariness.

Zeitgeist (G). Spirit of the times.

Boys Names

Here are the meanings and derivations of some of the more common boy's names. Diminutives have not been included—for example Eddie, Ned and Teddy are not listed as they have the same meaning as Edward.

Adam (Hebrew): "man of earth."
Adrian (Latin): "man of the seacoast."
Alan (Celtic): "harmony, cheerful."
Albert (Teutonic): "noble and bright."
Alexander (Greek): "protector of men."
Alfred (Anglo-Saxon): "wise as an elf, counsellor."
Andrew (Greek): "manly."
Anthony (Latin): "worthy; strong."
Arthur (Celtic): "strong as a rock."
Bernard (Teutonic): "grim bear."
Brian (Celtic): "strong; powerful."
Charles (Teutonic): "man."
Christopher (Greek): "Christ-bearer."
Colin (Celtic): "dove."
Craig (Celtic): "of the crag or stony hill."
Cyril (Greek): "Lord."
Daniel (Hebrew): "the Lord is judge."
David (Hebrew): "beloved."
Dennis (Greek): "lover of fine wines."
Derek (Teutonic): "the people's ruler."
Desmond (Celtic): "worldly; sophisticated."
Donald (Celtic): "proud chief."
Douglas (Celtic): "dark grey; from the dark stream."
Edgar (Angle-Saxon): "lucky spear; fortunate warrior."
Edmund (Anglo-Saxon): "fortunate or rich protector."
Edward (Anglo-Saxon): "prosperous guardian."
Eric (Teutonic): "kingly."
Ernest (Teutonic): "sincere; earnest."
Francis (Teutonic): "free."

100

Frederick (Teutonic): "peaceful ruler."
Gary (Anglo-Saxon): "mighty spear."
Geoffrey (Teutonic): "God's peace; peace of the land."
George (Greek): "farmer; tiller of the soil."
Gerald (Teutonic): "firm spearman."
Gilbert (Teutonic): "bright pledge."
Gordon (Anglo-Saxon): "from the cornered hill."
Graham (Teutonic): "from the grey home."
Gregory (Greek): "vigilant."
Guy (French): "guide; leader."
Harold (Anglo-Saxon): "powerful warrior."
Henry (Teutonic): "home ruler."
Herbert (Teutonic): "bright warrior."
James (Hebrew): "the supplanter."
Jeremy (Hebrew): "exalted by the Lord."
John (Hebrew): "God's gracious gift."
Joseph (Hebrew): "He shall add."
Keith (Celtic): "a place."
Kenneth (Celtic): "handsome."
Kevin (Celtic): "kind; gentle."
Lawrence (Latin): "laurel; crowned with laurel."
Leonard (Latin): "lion; brave as a lion."
Leslie (Celtic): "from the grey fort."
Louis, Lewis (Teutonic): "renowned in battle."
Malcolm (Celtic): "servant."
Mark, Martin (Latin): "belonging to Mars; a warrior."
Matthew (Hebrew): "God's gift."
Maurice (Latin): "dark; Moorish."
Michael (Hebrew): "Godlike."
Neville (Latin): "from the new town."
Nicholas (Greek): "victory of the people."
Nigel (Latin): "dark; black."
Noel (Latin): "Christmas."
Oliver (Latin): "olive; peace."
Patrick (Latin): "noble; patrician."
Paul (Latin): "small."

Peter (Greek): "rock."

Philip (Greek): "lover of horses."

Randolph, (Anglo-Saxon): "protected; advised by wolves."

Raymond (Teutonic): "wise protection."

Reginald (Teutonic): "powerful judgement."

Richard (Teutonic): "powerful king."

Robert (Teutonic): "of shining fame."

Rodney (Teutonic): "renowned."

Roland (Teutonic): "fame of the land."

Rudolph (Teutonic): "famed wolf."

Samuel (Hebrew): "asked of God."

Sidney (French): "a follower of St. Denis."

Simon (Hebrew): "hearer."

Stanley (Slavonic): "pride of the camp."

Stephen (Greek): "crowned."

Stewart (Anglo-Saxon): "keeper of the estate."

Terence (Latin): "tender."

Thomas (Hebrew): "a twin."

Timothy (Greek): "honouring God."

Vernon (Latin): "growing green; flourishing."

Victor (Latin): "the conqueror."

Vincent (Latin): "the conqueror."

Walter (Teutonic): "powerful warrior."

Wilfred (Teutonic): "firm peacemaker."

William (Teutonic): "helmet of resolution."

PEOPLE AND SCIENCE

Nowadays a higher proportion of people than ever before live in well-built houses, have enough to eat, are well clothed and have at birth an expectation of life of some sixty to seventy years. Two centuries ago this expectation of life was not much more than half the present figure, for lack of medical knowledge together with poor living conditions resulted in much ill health and in epidemics which wiped out huge sections of the population at a single stroke.

Science has changed all this—through researches in medicine and agriculture, by finding ways to make the things we need more rapidly and more cheaply and by discovering new substances out of which we can construct the complicated machinery of the modern world.

Here are some of the techniques developed by science in the past two centuries.

Brick-making by Machine

Most countries have clay suitable for brick-making. This is dug out of the ground by mechanical shovels, then fed into a system of huge rollers which crush it into a fine, powdery substance. Moisture is added, and a band of clay is forced through a hole and then cut into individual bricks by wires. The wet bricks are slowly dried, then put in a kiln and baked at a high temperature.

Cement Manufacture

Modern building technique is very largely dependent on cement. Clay, chalk and limestone are crushed, then fed into a machine which mixes them with water into a thick cream.

This cream, known as 'slurry', is conveyed to a high-temperature kiln which reduces it to clinker. The clinker passes between a series of rollers which grind it up, and the pale grey powder which results is cement. For building purposes this is mixed in a revolving drum with sand and water, using proportions of from three to five shovels of sand to each shovel of cement. For concrete, up to six shovels of 'aggregate' (a mixture of sand and small stones) is used with each shovel of cement.

Electric Power

This is produced by using water power, some form of fuel, or atomic energy (see section on **Nuclear Power**). The pressure of water from a dam, or, alternatively, steam created by burning fuel, turns a dynamo. The rotation of this spins a rotor. The rotor is an electro-magnet, which, surrounded by a coil of wire, sets up an electric current in the wire.

Gas Production

Still the principal source of heat for household cooking, gas is made by baking coal in a container or retort. The gas given off is stored in gasometers until required. By-products of the process include petrol, acids, drugs, perfumes, dyes, tar and coke. Natural gas from the North Sea is being used in Britain for commercial and domestic purposes.

Glass-making

The method of glass manufacture has changed little over the centuries, but the speed and mechanisation have been geatly increased. Specially selected sand is mixed with limestone and soda ash and melted until liquid. It is then rolled out to make plate glass, moulded to make the cheaper kind of jars, tumblers and bottles, or blown into shape for high-quality articles. Glass-blowing is still done by hand; the blower dips a long tube into the molten glass, then blows through the tube as if inflating a balloon.

Paper Manufacture

The tremendous output of books and newspapers today means that many thousands of tons of paper have to be made every year. What was once a laborious process carried out by hand is now a highly mechanised industry. Paper is made of esparto grass, rag, wood-pulp or various mixtures of these materials. These are reduced to a fibrous pulp, boiled, and bleached. The pulp then travels along a moving belt over a suction chamber which removes excess moisture. The sheet which is formed through this process goes between rollers and drying cylinders until it emerges as a roll of white paper.

Printing

Modern printing has come a long way since 1474 when William Caxton printed the first book in the English language. Today millions of newspapers, magazines and books are produced on fast, modern printing machines. Three main methods of printing are used. The first, probably the oldest, is called Letterpress. This involves raised metal letters or characters. Ink is applied and the paper pressed onto them. This book is printed by Letterpress.

The second method, also very old in origin, has been developed extensively only in the last twenty years. This is called Offset Lithography and employs a photographically prepared plate which is inked. Because of the way it is made, only the areas which are required to print accept the ink. This then prints onto a rubber covered cylinder which in turn prints, or offsets, onto the paper.

The third method, Gravure, is used mainly for magazine printing. Small holes of varying depth are etched into a plate. This is first inked. A special blade called a 'doctor blade' scrapes away the unwanted surface ink leaving only that which is trapped in the holes. Paper is then pressed against the plate and the ink is drawn out on to it.

The two types of printing machines used are sheet-fed and rotary. Sheet-fed is used mainly for books, and prints the sheets of paper one at a time. Rotary is mainly used for newspapers, printing a continuous reel of paper, which is cut and folded afterwards.

Spinning

Two hundred years of progress in spinning have speeded up the process rather than changed the method. The original spinning-wheel produced one thread at a time. The wool, after washing, carding to remove lumps and combing to place the hairs in one direction, was twisted and rolled into yarn. The modern spinning machine does this to hundreds of threads at the same time.

Steel Manufacture

To make steel from cast iron it is necessary to remove certain substances which exist in it as impurities, the chief of which is carbon. The method of removal is generally by means of an open-hearth furnace, in which pigs, or bars, of cast iron, are raised to a great heat by burning gas and air fed into the hearth at high pressure. The molten steel is poured into moulds, and the ingots thus made pass between rollers which press them into girders.

Water Supply and Drainage

Water as it comes from most rivers is not pure enough to

drink. Also, we cannot depend on a river for supplies at all times of the year. The solutions to these two problems are purification and the use of reservoirs. River water, pumped into a reservoir, is taken out as required and placed in tanks containing purifying chemicals. From these, it flows to open tanks in which there are layers of gravel that filter away impurities. The final stage involves the addition of still more chemicals, and the water is then kept in covered tanks and reservoirs until pumped through the mains to individual houses.

Hot water is produced in the modern house by one of three methods: gas, electricity or solid fuel. In the first method, water is led over powerful burners, usually by means of a spiral tube, so that while the outlet tap is running the water is receiving heat from the burners. Water is warmed electrically by means of an immersion heater, which is an electric heating element, protected by a tube, placed inside a water tank. Heating water by a solid fuel stove requires an enclosed fire containing a water-jacket or an open fire with a back-boiler device. From the cold-water tank in the loft, water runs down to the hot-water tank (often in a cupboard), and from there down a pipe to the bottom of the water-jacket. As the fire heats the water it rises up a second pipe to the hot-water tank. It is replaced automatically by colder water coming down the first pipe, and the circulation provides a constant supply of hot water in the tank from which yet another pipe leads out, at the top, to supply the hot taps in the kitchen and bathroom.

Our modern drainage system is just as important as our water supply. In the past, refuse was thrown into open drains in the streets. Insects and germs breeding in these drains spread disease. Modern sewers all run below ground. The 'U' tube under the sink, bath and W.C., in which water always remains, prevents gases and unpleasant smells from coming up from the sewers into which the waste pipes lead. When the sewage reaches the sewage farm it is mechanically sieved to remove grit which is later used for concrete and road-works. Then the solids are separated from the liquids in settling tanks. The liquids are agitated by a jet of compressed air, which makes the bacteria multiply rapidly and breaks down any remaining solids into small particles. The final products are a harmless liquid which can be released into a river or the sea, and mud which, when fermented, gives off a gas that supplies the main source of power of the sewage farm.

The following inventions have also done much to change the world in recent times.

Camera

Light entering a darkened box through a small hole will project an image inside the box of the scene outside—but in reverse and upside-down. In practice a lens with a shutter is used instead of a small hole, in order to admit more light. A sensitised plate or film at the back of the camera receives the impression. The film or plate is then removed in a dark room, where it is immersed in chemical solutions. This process produces a negative, with its black objects white and *vice versa*. A positive, or print, is made by placing the negative on sensitised paper and exposing it to the light, whereupon the white portions of the negative admit light. The sensitised paper is then treated with chemicals, and the original image appears.

Diesel Engine

This is a very high compression internal combustion engine. Air is drawn into a cylinder and compressed to about five hundred pounds per square inch. This raises its temperature to a point where, when fuel oil is pumped in, it immediately ignites and creates the explosion necessary to force the piston down.

Internal Combustion Engine

This is the name for the petrol engine used in cars, motorcycles and light lorries. A carburettor converts petrol into a fine vapour, and also draws in air which mixes with it. The mixture travels through a valve system into the top of a cylinder and is there exploded under pressure by means of an electric sparking plug. The explosion forces down the piston, from which a connecting rod runs to a crank-shaft. On its return stroke the piston pushes out the burned gases through the valve system; its next journey down draws in a fresh supply of fuel, and its upward journey compresses the fuel in readiness for the next explosion.

Jet Engine

Turbojet. Modern aircraft are frequently fitted with turbojet engines, as they develop far greater power than piston engines. They run on paraffin, which is burned with compressed air to produce expanding gases which drive the blades of a turbine. On the same axle another turbine forces air into the firing chamber. The turbojet propels by forcing out a jet of hot air at its rear. The turboprop, a later development, uses its turbine to turn an air-screw.

Ramjet. This is an engine intended to 'take over' an aircraft once it has reached a speed of roughly two hundred miles an hour. Air is forced in at the nose of the engine, fuel is burned in it, and the resultant high pressure produces a propellent exhaust. The ramjet becomes more efficient as it gains speed, for speed adds to the intake of air and therefore to the potential thrust.

Hovercraft

Though neither an aircraft nor a boat, this British invention is an entirely new form of transport. Basically, it is a round boat with a flat bottom. In the centre of the vehicle is an engine which drives air down through the bottom of the boat. For this air to escape, it must raise the hull. Hence the hovering. To travel forward, another engine (either jet or more normally rotor bladed) is used. The Hovercraft is limited in its uses as it can travel across only fairly smooth land or water. However, its first commercial test came when Hovercrafts were ordered by a fruit company to transport bananas across previously inaccessible swampland. As the engines are increased in efficiency, they will allow the Hovercraft to travel higher above the ground and therefore clear larger waves or land obstacles. They are now in use for passengers and cars between Britain and France, and also between the mainland and the Isle of Wight.

Plastics

There are two types—thermosetting and thermoplastic. The latter can be reshaped by the application of heat, but the former are subjected to heat during manufacture, and once moulded cannot be altered in shape. Thermoplastics include acrylic, vinyl and polystyrene—all in common use for household purposes and in toy-making. Many plastics are formed by treating coal derivatives such as phenol.

Steam Locomotion

Basically, the modern steam locomotive uses the same system as George Stephenson's original *Rocket*. Coal or oil is burned to produce fierce heat and create super-heated steam. This passes in controlled quantities to the cylinders, in turn pushing the pistons back and forth by being admitted to each cylinder first at one end and then at the other. This backwards and forwards movement is converted into a circular movement by connecting rods joined off-centre to the main driving wheels of the locomotive, and is passed from one main wheel to the next by coupling rods.

Submarine

The main sea-weapon in any future war would probably be the submarine, because of its proved worth in disrupting supply lines by sinking merchant ships and also because it is an ideal launching platform for short-range guided missiles. The principle of the submarine is that of double-shell construction. The crew's quarters and the engine rooms are in an airtight shell, and between this and the outer shell are diving tanks. To submerge the submarine, these tanks are flooded by opening a series of valves. To return to the surface, powerful pumps are used to clear the tanks.

Propulsion is by diesel engine, battery-driven electric motors and, recently, nuclear power.

Great Inventions and Discoveries

Discovery or Invention	Person Responsible	Country	Year
Aeroplane	Wilbur and Orville Wright	United States	1903
Airship	Henri Giffard	France	1852
Atomic Structure	Lord Rutherford	Britain	1910–11
Balloon	Joseph and Jacques Montgolfier	France	1783
Barometer	Evangelista Toricelli	Italy	1643
Bathysphere	W. Bebbe	United States	1934

Bicycle	Kirkpatrick MacMillan	Britain	1839
Clock, Pendulum	Christiaan Huygens	Netherlands	1656
Diesel Engine	Rudolf Diesel	Germany	1897
Dynamite	Alfred Nobel	Sweden	1867
Dynamo	Michael Faraday	Britain	1831
Electric Arc Lamp	Sir Humphry Davy	Britain	1809
Electric Battery	Alessandro Volta	Italy	1800
Electric Lamp, carbon filament	Thomas Edison	United States	1879
Engine, internal combustion (gas)	Etienne Lenoir	France	1860
Engine, internal combustion (petrol)	Gottlieb Daimler	Germany	1883
Engine, Jet	Frank Whittle	Britain	1930
Gas Lighting	William Murdock	Britain	1792
Gramophone	Thomas A. Edison	United States	1877
Gyroscope	Jean Foncault	France	1852
Helicopter	Louis G. Bréguet	France	1909
Hovercraft	C.S. Cockerell	Britain	1955
Lift	Elisha Otis	United States	1852
Lightning Conductor	Benjamin Franklin	United States	1752
Locomotive, Steam	Richard Trevithick	Britain	1801
Machine Gun	Richard Gatling	United States	1862
Match, Friction	John Walker	Britain	1827
Match, Safety	J. E. Lundstrom	Sweden	1855
Microscope, Compound	Zacharias Janssen	Netherlands	1590
Motion-picture Camera	William Friese-Greene	Britain	1888
Motor-car	Karl Benz	Germany	1885

112

Nylon	W. H. Carothers	United States	1938
Parachute	J. P. Blanchard	France	1785
Penicillin	Sir Alexander Fleming	Britain	1929
Photography	J. Nicéphore Niepce	France	1822
Pianoforte	Bartolommeo Cristofori	Italy	1709
Pneumatic Tyre	Robert Thompson	Britain	1845
Postage Stamp	Sir Rowland Hill	Britain	1840
Power Loom	Edmund Cartwright	Britain	1786
Printing, Movable Type	Johann Gutenberg	Germany	c. 1440
Radar	Robert Watson-Watt	Britain	1935
Radio Telescope	Karl Jansky	United States	1931
Radium	Pierre and Marie Curie	France	1898
Safety Lamp, Miner's	Sir Humphry Davy	Britain	1816
Safety Pin	Walter Hunt	United States	1849
Sewing Machine	Walter Hunt	United States	1832
Sextant	John Hadley	Britain	1731
Steam Engine	James Watt	Britain	1769
Steam Locomotive	Richard Trevithick	Britain	1803
Steam Turbine	Sir Charles A. Parsons	Britain	1884
Stethoscope	René Laennec	France	1816
Tank	Sir Ernest Swinton	Britain	1914
Telephone	Alexander Graham Bell	United States	1876
Telescope, Refracting	Hans Lippershey	Netherlands	1608
Telescope, Reflecting	Isaac Newton	Britain	1669

Television	James Logie Baird	Britain	1926
Torpedo	Robert		
(Modern)	Whitehead	Britain	1868
Transistor	Bardeen, Brattain and Shockley	United States	1948
Typewriter	Christopher Sholes	United States	1868
Umbrella	Samuel Fox	Britain	1852
Vaccination	Edward Jenner	Britain	1796
Wireless Telegraphy	Guglielmo Marconi	Italy	1895
X-rays	Wilhelm Roentgen	Germany	1895

Journeys into Space

We live in the age of man's fastest scientific progress. His curiosity takes him to the Poles, to the deepest parts of the ocean and many miles high into the sky.

What is the sum total so far in the exploration of space—and what may lie ahead within your own lifetime?

The first space probes were the two Russian satellites, *Sputnik I*, and *Sputnik II*, in 1957, which were propelled by multiple-stage rockets to a distance of several hundred miles above the earth's surface, and then directed into orbit so that they circled the earth on a definite course at a speed of about 18,000 miles (29,000 km) per hour.

The Americans launched their first satellites in the early part of 1958, and then, in October, fired a multiple-stage rocket designed to explore the Moon. It was equipped with television gear and it was hoped that it would send back a picture of the far side of the Moon—the side which had never been seen by man.

This was a failure; at some 80,000 feet (24,000m) the flight ended and the object returned to the earth's atmosphere.

In September 1959, the Russian rocket *Lunik II* reached the Moon and photographed its far side.

In August 1960, another Russian rocket was put into orbit containing two dogs. This satellite reached its target back on Earth with the dogs unharmed. In the spring of 1961, the Americans made a similarly successful flight with a chimpanzee.

Then on 12 April of that year came the first man in space, when the Russians sent up Major Yuri Gagarin who made one orbit of the world before landing. This was improved on when fellow-Russian Major Gherman Titov made 17 orbits on August 6, 1961.

Much of America's space prestige was restored when they sent up their first astronaut on February 20, 1962, Colonel John Glenn making three orbits in his *Friendship 7*. This was followed by another three-orbit flight by Major Scott Carpenter in his space capsule *Aurora 7*. Since then, further flights in space have been carried out successfully, unmanned rockets have been fired to the Moon, and information satellites have been launched. In 1965, *Mariner IV* (U.S.A.) sent back to Earth close-up pictures of the surface of Mars, and Major Virgil Grissom (first man to fly twice in space) and Lt. Cdr. John Young completed a two-man American space mission, manoeuvring their craft's height and direction in orbit for the first time. On 15 December, 1965, America's *Gemini VI* and *VII* effected the first-ever human meeting in space. Meanwhile, also in 1965, Col. Belyaev piloted a two-man Russian spaceship while his companion, Lt. Col. Leonov, became the first man to walk into space, floating at the end of a 15 ft. (4·5 m) lifeline for 20 minutes.

In 1967, both American and Russian space probes landed on the Moon and sent information about its surface back to the Earth.

The American space programme reached its climax in July 1969 when the huge *Saturn* V rocket blasted off from Cape Kennedy carrying *Apollo XI* and the three-man crew, Neil Armstrong, Edwin Aldrin and Michael Collins. In the early hours of 21 July, Neil Armstrong became the first human being to set foot on the Moon. He was followed by Aldrin, while Collins piloted the command module orbiting above.

America's 1971 *Apollo 15* mission to the Moon proved an enormous success. That same year the Russians also made a major breakthrough when *Soyuz 11* docked with the *Salyut* space station. This proved the feasiblity of space stations orbiting for long periods, manned by a succession of astronauts and scientists. The Americans then launched Skylab in 1972, an experimental venture in their plans for space stations. In 1975 came the first American—Russian link-up in space.

Nuclear Power and its Peaceful Uses

Nuclear power—born of the research which made the first atomic bomb—is now being harnessed for peaceful uses and will change man's whole pattern of living. But what is nuclear power, and how do we make it work for us?

It was a New Zealand scientist working in Britain, Lord Rutherford, who did much of the pioneer research which revealed the enormous power dormant in the nucleus of the atom—power enough to provide the world with unlimited resources, power which could heat every house and factory in the world, pump water to every desert on the globe and turn every machine-wheel man can create. His problem was how to release that power and how to do so safely.

What is an atom? The nuclear theory of the atom, which was put forward by Rutherford and his colleague Sir Joseph Thomson, was published as long ago as 1911. The atom consists of a minutely small but very heavy nucleus containing a positive electric charge; round this circulate much lighter electrons having a total negative electric charge which exactly equals the positive charge of the nucleus. In 1932 Sir James Chadwick discovered that the nucleus consists of protons, which are electrically positive, and neutrons, which are neutral.

116

How does power come into all this? All matter is made up of atoms of elements, and certain elements have atoms which are known as 'unstable'—meaning that the nucleus can be upset, giving off a tremendous amount of power. Once started, this process can be continued in what is known as a controlled chain reaction, providing a steady supply of power in the form of heat.

An atomic pile, or power unit, is made up of carbon blocks in which are placed rods of the unstable element, uranium. Control of the heat is maintained by means of other rods, of boron or cadmium, either of which has the effect of slowing down nuclear reaction. These rods can be raised or lowered in the pile to regulate its output as the temperature drops or increases.

Putting the heat to practical use is done by forcing carbon dioxide through the pile by means of pumps. The gas emerges at high temperature and operates steam turbine generators which supply electricity to the National Grid.

The world's first economically practical atomic generator was put into use in Britain at Calder Hall, in 1956, and since then generators of various patterns, but operating on the same basic principles, have been working in the United States and Russia. Countries with less money and smaller industrial resources have formed groups such as the European Organisation for Nuclear Research, to provide themselves with the equipment to carry out their own experiments towards more advanced systems of developing atomic power. But the story of nuclear power does not end with the setting up of hundreds of generators throughout the world to make us independent of coal and oil. Generators which depend on uranium to provide the active heart of the pile are expensive, as uranium is a rare metal. The next step is cheap nuclear power, and this seems likely to come from a hydrogen reactor. As the atomic reactor depends on the principle of the atomic bomb—fission—the hydrogen reactor depends on that of the hydrogen bomb, which is fusion. It is actually the fusion of light elements into heavier ones which produces the power in this case. The principle is the one which provides the sun's energy. Scientists hope to produce hydrogen reactors costing little to run and yielding electric power direct, without turbines and generators.

If they succeed, man will truly have achieved a limitless source of useful power.

Anatomy

Like big buildings the body is constructed round a framework of girders. To this frame or skeleton all the muscles and important organs are attached.

The backbone (spine) is made up of ring-like bones, and down the middle runs the spinal cord. At the top of the spine is the head, which is like a bone box protecting the brain.

Attached to the spine is a cage of bones, the ribs, which protect the heart, lungs and liver. These ribs are joined at the front to the breast-bone.

To this breast-bone are joined the two collar-bones, and to these the two shoulder-blades and to these the arms.

At the lower end of the spine is the pelvis, to which are attached the legs.

The upper arms and thighs have one bone each; the forearms and lower legs, two bones each. The wrists and ankles contain groups of small square bones. Longer ones are in the palms and soles of the feet, and not quite such long ones in the fingers and toes.

There are seven major organs which carry out the various functions of the body.

The brain directs the body's working by receiving messages through the nervous system and by sending messages to other parts of the body along the spinal cord and nerves.

The heart pumps the blood through the body by way of the arteries, and receives it back through the veins.

The lungs take air into the body by means of the upper

118

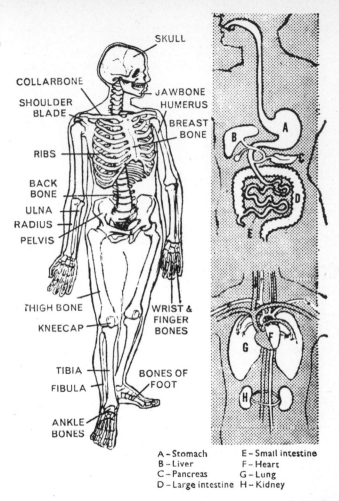

SKULL

COLLARBONE

SHOULDER BLADE

JAWBONE
HUMERUS

BREAST BONE

RIBS

BACK BONE

ULNA
RADIUS
PELVIS

THIGH BONE

KNEECAP

WRIST & FINGER BONES

TIBIA
FIBULA

BONES OF FOOT

ANKLE BONES

A – Stomach
B – Liver
C – Pancreas
D – Large intestine

E – Small intestine
F – Heart
G – Lung
H – Kidney

119

respiratory tract. They also expel carbon dioxide, a waste product taken from the blood.

The stomach takes in food, begins the digestive process and sends the food through the intestines to complete digestion.

The liver and the pancreas discharge juices into the small intestine which aid in the digestion of food. The liver also stores vitamins, and aids in purifying the blood, while the pancreas regulates the amount of sugar in the blood.

The kidneys remove waste materials from the blood. These waste materials are carried to the bladder, where they are kept until evacuated from the body.

Weights and Measures

Weights. Imperial System (used in Britain and certain Commonwealth lands, but being replaced gradually by the metric system).

Avoirdupois Weight

27.34	grains	=	1 dram
16	drams	=	1 ounce
16	ounces	=	1 pound
14	pounds	=	1 stone
28	pounds	=	1 quarter
4	quarters	=	1 hundredweight
20	hundredweights	=	1 ton

Troy Weight (used by jewellers)

3.17	grains	=	1 carat
24	grains	=	1 pennyweight
20	pennyweights	=	1 ounce
12	ounces	=	1 pound
100	pounds	=	1 hundredweight

Apothecaries' Weight

20 grains	=	1 scruple
3 scruples	=	1 drachm
8 drachms	=	1 ounce
12 ounces	=	1 pound

Weights. Metric System

10 milligrammes	=	1 centigramme
10 centigrammes	=	1 decigramme
10 decigrammes	=	1 gramme
10 grammes	=	1 decagramme
10 decagrammes	=	1 hectogramme
10 hectogrammes	=	1 kilogramme
10 kilogrammes	=	1 myriagramme
10 myriagrammes	=	1 quintal
10 quintals	=	1 metric tonne

Weight Conversions

Imperial		Metric	
1 grain	=	0.0648	grammes
1 dram	=	1.772	grammes
1 ounce	=	28.3495	grammes
1 pound	=	0.4536	kilogrammes
1 stone	=	6.35	kilogrammes
1 quarter	=	12.7	kilogrammes
1 hundredweight	=	50.8	kilogrammes
1 ton	=	1,016	kilogrammes
		or 1.016	metric tonnes
Metric		Imperial	
1 milligramme	=	0.015	grains
1 centigramme	=	0.154	grains
1 decigramme	=	1.543	grains
1 gramme	=	15.432	grains

121

1 decagramme	=	5.644	drams
1 hectogramme	=	3.527	ounces
1 kilogramme	=	2.205	pounds
1 myriagramme	=	22.046	pounds
1 quintal	=	1.968	hundredweights
1 metric tonne	=	0.9842	tons

Measures. Imperial System

Linear Measure

12	inches	=	1 foot
3	feet	=	1 yard
5½	yards	=	1 rod, pole or perch
22	yards	=	1 chain
10	chains	=	1 furlong
8	furlongs	=	1 mile
			(1,760 yards; 5,280 feet)
3	miles	=	1 league

Square Measure

144	square inches	=	1 square foot
9	square feet	=	1 square yard
30¼	square yards	=	1 square rod, pole or perch
40	square rods	=	1 rood
4	roods (4,840 square yards)	=	1 acre
640	acres	=	1 square mile

Capacity Measure

| 4 | gills | = | 1 pint |
| 2 | pints | = | 1 quart |

4	quarts	=	1 gallon (0.833 Imperial gallons = 1 U.S. gallon)
2	gallons	=	1 peck
4	pecks	=	1 bushel
8	bushels	=	1 quarter
4¼	quarters	=	1 chaldron

Cubic Measure

1,728 cubic inches	=	1 cubic foot
27 cubic feet	=	1 cubic yard

Measures. Metric System

Linear Measure

10 millimetres	=	1 centimetre
10 centimetres	=	1 decimetre
10 decimetres	=	1 metre
10 metres	=	1 decametre
10 decametres	=	1 hectometre
10 hectometres	=	1 kilometre
10 kilometres	=	1 myriametre

Square Measure

100 square millimetres	=	1 square centimetre
100 square centimetres	=	1 square decimetre
100 square decimetres	=	1 square metre
100 square metres	=	1 are
100 ares	=	1 hectare
100 hectares	=	1 square kilometre

Cubic Measure

1,000 cubic millimetres	=	1 cubic centimetre
1,000 cubic centimetres	=	1 cubic decimetre
1,000 cubic decimetres	=	1 cubic metre

Capacity Measure

10 millilitres	=	1 centilitre
10 centilitres	=	1 decilitre
10 decilitres	=	1 litre
10 litres	=	1 decalitre
10 decalitres	=	1 hectolitre
10 hectolitres	=	1 kilolitre

Measure Conversions

Linear Measure

Imperial		Metric	
1 inch	=	2.54	centimetres
1 foot	=	30.48	centimetres
1 yard	=	0.9144	metres
1 rod	=	5.029	metres
1 chain	=	20.117	metres
1 furlong	=	201.168	metres
1 mile	=	1.6093	kilometres

Metric		Imperial	
1 millimetre	=	0.03937	inches
1 centimetre	=	0.39370	inches
1 decimetre	=	3.93701	inches
1 metre	=	39.3701	inches
		(1.09361	yards)

1 decametre	=	10.9361	yards
1 hectometre	=	109.361	yards
1 kilometre	=	0.62137	miles

Square Measure

Imperial | | | Metric

1 square inch	=	6.4516	square centimetres
1 square foot	=	9.29	square decimetres
1 square yard	=	0.836	square metres
1 square rod	=	25.293	square metres
1 rood	=	10.117	ares
1 acre	=	0.405	hectares
1 square mile	=	259	hectares

Metric | | | Imperial

1 square centimetre	=	0.155	square inches
1 square metre	=	10.764	square feet
		(1.196	square yards)
1 are	=	119.6	square yards
1 hectare	=	2.47	acres

Cubic Measure

Imperial | | | Metric

1 cubic inch	=	16.387	cubic centimetres
1 cubic foot	=	0.0283	cubic metres
1 cubic yard	=	0.7646	cubic metres

Metric | | | Imperial

| 1 cubic centimetre | = | 0.061 | cubic inches |

1 cubic decimetre	=	61.024	cubic inches
1 cubic metre	=	35.315	cubic feet
		(1.308	cubic yards)

Capacity Measure

Imperial   Metric

1 gill	=	1.42	decilitres
1 pint	=	0.568	litres
1 quart	=	1.136	litres
1 gallon	=	4.546	litres
1 bushel	=	36.37	litres
1 quarter	=	2.91	hectolitres

Metric   Imperial

1 centilitre	=	0.07	gills
1 decilitre	=	0.176	pints
1 litre	=	1.7598	pints
1 decalitre	=	2.2	gallons
1 hectolitre	=	2.75	bushels
		(21.99	gallons)

Nautical Measures

6 feet	=	1 fathom
100 fathoms	=	1 cable
10 cables (6,080 feet)	=	1 nautical mile
		(1,852 metres)
1 knot	=	1 nautical mile *per hour*

Other Measures

1 tablespoon	=	$\frac{1}{2}$ fluid ounce
1 dessertspoon	=	$\frac{1}{4}$ fluid ounce
1 teaspoon	=	$\frac{1}{8}$ fluid ounce

Miscellaneous

1 gallon of water weighs 10 pounds.
1 horsepower is the power required to raise 550 pounds by
1 foot in 1 second.
1 kilowatt is the power required to raise 737.6 pounds by
1 foot in 1 second.

Measure and Sizes for Paper

A0	841 × 1189 mm
A1	594 × 841 mm
A2	420 × 594 mm
A3	297 × 420 mm
A4	210 × 297 mm
RA0	860 × 1220 mm
RA1	610 × 860 mm
RA2	430 × 610 mm
SRA0	900 × 1280 mm
SRA1	640 × 900 mm
SRA2	450 × 640 mm
Metric Quad Crown	768 × 1008 mm
Metric Quad Large Crown	816 × 1056 mm
Metric Quad Demy	888 × 1128 mm
Metric Quad Royal	960 × 1272 mm

Thermometer Readings

The three systems for marking thermometers are Celsius
(the Centigrade scale), Fahrenheit and Réaumur. Celsius,
which shows 0° for freezing and 100° for boiling water, is
used throughout the world for scientific purposes; it is used
for general purposes in Europe. Fahrenheit, in which 32° is
the freezing temperature and 212° the boiling temperature of
water, is the scale previously used in Britain (now transferring

to the Centigrade scale) and still employed in the United States. Réaumur, with 0° for freezing and 80° for boiling water, is nearly obsolete, but is occasionally found in old books of European origin on scientific matters and cookery.

A comparison of Celsius and Fahrenheit scales follows:

Celsius		Fahrenheit
—40	=	—40
—30	=	—22
—25	=	—13
—20	=	—4
—17.8	=	0
—15	=	5
—10	=	14
—5	=	23
0	=	32
5	=	41
10	=	50
15	=	59
20	=	68
25	=	77
30	=	86
35	=	95
40	=	104
45	=	113
50	=	122
55	=	131
60	=	140
70	=	158
80	=	176
90	=	194
100	=	212

To change Celsius to Fahrenheit, multiply by 9, divide by 5 and add 32.

128

To change Fahrenheit to Celsius, subtract 32, multiply by 5 and divide by 9.

Normal blood temperature in human beings is 36.9 °C (98.4 °F).

Roman Numerals

I =	1
II =	2
III =	3
IV =	4
V =	5
VI =	6
VII =	7
VIII =	8
IX =	9
X =	10
XI =	11
XII =	12
XIII =	13
XIV =	14
XV =	15
XVI =	16
XVII =	17
XVIII =	18
XIX =	19
XX =	20
XXX =	30
XL =	40
L =	50
LX =	60
LXX =	70
LXXX =	80
XC =	90
C =	100

CC =		200
CCC =		300
CD =		400
D =		500
DC =		600
DCC =		700
DCCC =		800
CM =		900
M =		1,000
MM =		2,000
MMM =		3,000
MV̄ =		4,000
V̄ =		5,000
X̄ =		10,000
L̄ =		50,000
C̄ =		100,000
D̄ =		500,000
M̄ =		1,000,000
MCMLXXIV =		1974

Common Formulae

Circumference of Circle	=	$2\pi r$ (π = 3.1416; r = radius)
Area of Circle	=	πr^2
Volume of Sphere	=	$\frac{4}{3}\pi r^3$
Surface of Sphere	=	$4\pi r^2$
Volume of Cylinder	=	$\pi r^2 h$ (h = height)

Specific Gravity

Glass	=	2.4—2.6
Brass	=	8.1—8.6
Iron	=	8.95
Copper	=	8.95

Silver	=	10.3—10.5
Mercury	=	13.596

Coefficients of Expansion

Glass	=	0.000022
Iron	=	0.000033—0.000044
Copper	=	0.000051
Brass	=	0.000053—0.000057
Gases	=	0.00366

Boiling Points at 760 mm Pressure

Nitrous Oxide	—87.90°C
Chlorine	—33.60°C
Ammonia	—33.50°C
Ether	33.00°C
Chloroform	60.20°C
Alcohol	78.30°C
Benzene	80.40°C
Distilled Water	100.00°C
Sulphuric Acid	325.00°C
Mercury	357.25°C
Sulphur	444.70°C

Speed of Sound

Medium	Feet per Second	Metres per Second
Through Air at 0°C	1,090	332
Through Water	4,758	1.450
Through Carbon Dioxide	850	259
Through Hydrogen	4,160	1.268
Through Glass	approx. 16,500	5.030

Chemical Names of Everyday Substances

Substance	Chemical Name
Alcohol	Ethyl Alcohol
Alum	Aluminium Potassium Sulphate
Baking Powder	Sodium Bicarbonate
Boracic Acid	Boric Acid
Borax	Sodium Borate
Chalk	Calcium Carbonate
Common Salt	Sodium Chloride
Epsom Salts	Magnesium Sulphate
Fire-damp	Methane
Glauber Salts	Sodium Sulphate
Hypo	Sodium Thiosulphate
Lime	Calcium Oxide
Magnesia	Magnesium Oxide
Plaster of Paris	Calcium Sulphate
Red Lead	Triplumbic Tetroxide
Sal Ammoniac	Ammonium Chloride
Saltpetre	Potassium Nitrate
Salts of Lemon	Potassium Hydrogen Oxalate
Sal Volatile	Ammonium Carbonate
Spirits of Salts	Hydrochloric Acid
Vinegar	Dilute Acetic Acid
Washing Soda	Crystalline Sodium Carbonate
White Lead	Basic Lead Carbonate

Table of Elements

Atomic No.	Element	Symbol	Atomic Weight
1	Hydrogen	H	1.008
2	Helium	He	4.003

3	Lithium	Li	6.399
4	Beryllium	Be	9
5	Boron	B	10.811
6	Carbon	C	12.011
7	Nitrogen	N	14.007
8	Oxygen	O	15.99
9	Fluorine	F	18.998
10	Neon	Ne	20.183
11	Sodium	Na	22.990
12	Magnesium	Mg	24.312
13	Aluminium	Al	26.982
14	Silicon	Si	28.086
15	Phosphorus	P	30.974
16	Sulphur	S	32.064
17	Chlorine	Cl	35.453
18	Argon	Ar	39.948
19	Potassium	K	39.102
20	Calcium	Ca	40.080
21	Scandium	Sc	44.956
22	Titanium	Ti	47.900
23	Vanadium	V	50.942
24	Chromium	Cr	51.996
25	Manganese	Mn	54.938
26	Iron	Fe	55.847
27	Cobalt	Co	58.933 ·
28	Nickel	Ni	58.710
29	Copper	Cu	63.546
30	Zinc	Zn	65.370
31	Gallium	Ga	69.720
32	Germanium	Ge	72.590
33	Arsenic	As	74.922
34	Selenium	Se	78.960
35	Bromine	Br	79.904
36	Krypton	Kr	83.800
37	Rubidium	Rb	85.470
38	Strontium	Sr	87.620

39	Yttrium	Y	88.905
40	Zirconium	Zr	91.220
41	Niobium	Nb	92.906
42	Molybdenum	Mo	95.940
43	Technetium	Tc	99.000
44	Ruthenium	Ru	101.700
45	Rhodium	Rh	102.905
46	Palladium	Pd	106.400
47	Silver	Ag	107.868
48	Cadmium	Cd	112.400
49	Indium	In	114.820
50	Tin	Sn	118.690
51	Antimony	Sb	121.750
52	Tellurium	Te	127.600
53	Iodine	I	126.904
54	Xenon	Xe	131.300
55	Caesium	Cs	132.905
56	Barium	Ba	137.340
57	Lanthanum	La	138.910
58	Cerium	Ce	140.120
59	Praseodymium	Pr	140.907
60	Neodymium	Nd	144.240
61	Promethium	Pm	145.000
62	Samarium	Sm	150.350
63	Europium	Eu	151.9
64	Gadolinium	Gd	157.250
65	Terbium	Tb	158.924
66	Dysprosium	Dy	162.500
67	Holmium	Ho	164.930
68	Erbium	Er	167.260
69	Thulium	Tm	168.93
70	Ytterbium	Yb	173.040
71	Lutetium	Lu	174.970
72	Hafnium	Hf	178.490
73	Tantalum	Ta	180.948
74	Tungsten	W	183.850

75	Rhenium	Re	186.200
76	Osmium	Os	190.200
77	Iridium	Ir	192.20
78	Platinum	Pt	195.090
79	Gold	Au	196.967
80	Mercury	Hg	200.590
81	Thallium	Tl	204.370
82	Lead	Pb	207.190
83	Bismuth	Bi	208.98
84	Polonium	Po	210.000
85	Astatine	At	210.000
86	Radon	Rn	222.000
87	Francium	Fr	223.000
88	Radium	Ra	226.000
89	Actinium	Ac	227.000
90	Thorium	Th	232.038
91	Protoactinium	Pa	231.000
92	Uranium	U	238.030
93	Neptunium	Np	237.000
94	Plutonium	Plu	242.000
95	Americium	Am	243.000
96	Curium	Cm	247.000
97	Berkelium	Bk	249.000
98	Californium	Cf	251.000
99	Einsteinium	Es	254.000
100	Fermium	Fm	253.000
101	Mendelevium	Md	258.000
102	Nobelium	No	253.000
103	Lawrencium	Lr	257.000

Chemical Indicators

Indicators show whether a substance is alkaline, acid or neutral. The following list gives the effect of adding an indicator.

Indicator	Alkaline	Acid	Neutral
Litmus	turns blue	turns red	turns purple
Methyl Orange	turns yellow	turns pink	remains orange

Wind Force

When weather forecasters want to inform ships of the exact strength of winds likely to blow in their areas, they do so by using the Beaufort Scale, referring to 'Force 2' or 'Force 5', or whatever is appropriate. The Scale is given overleaf...

Force Number	Description	M.P.H.
0	Calm	0 — 1
1	Light air	1 — 3
2	Light breeze	4 — 7
3	Gentle breeze	8 — 12
4	Moderate breeze	13 — 18
5	Fresh breeze	19 — 24
6	Strong breeze	25 — 31
7	Near gale	32 — 38
8	Gale	39 — 46
9	Strong gale	47 — 54
10	Storm	55 — 63
11	Violent storm	64 — 73
12	Hurricane	over 73

PEOPLE AND THE ARTS

Nowadays most of us are a little inclined to forget the importance of the arts in adding enjoyment and beauty to our lives and in shaping the world in which we live. Many people are inclined to dismiss great paintings as 'a lot of dry and dusty old pieces of canvas in museums', although the art of the great painters in the past has given us our skill in present-day industrial design, our knowledge of colours and our ability to make our own homes pleasant to look at and pleasant to live in.

As artists have changed the world we look at, so writers and philosophers have changed the way we think about the world. It would be impossible to imagine our world and the life we live without the influence of painters, writers and musicians.

Here are some of the leading artists, sculptors, musicians and writers of the past:

ADAM, *Robert (1728—1792).* Scottish architect who helped revive the handsome building styles of ancient Greece. Much of his work can still be seen in central London and in Edinburgh, where a large proportion of the 'New Town' was erected according to his designs.

ADDISON, *Joseph (1672—1719).* Leading writer and politician. He is remembered today as a writer of light and amusing essays for the journal called the *Spectator,* which he founded in partnership with Sir Richard Steele.

AESCHYLUS *(525—456 B.C.).* One of the leading playwrights of ancient Greece, he is regarded as the father of Greek tragedy. His plays have been translated into English and make interesting reading.

AESOP *(629—560 B.C.).* Greek slave who compiled a large collection of moral fables, many of which are as applicable today as they were when first told.

ANGELICO, Fra *(1387—1455)*. One of the greatest Italian Renaissance painters. Many of his finest pictures are in the galleries at Florence.

ARISTOPHANES *(450—385 B.C)*. Leading playwright of ancient Greece. Most of his plays are satirical and are still widely read and performed.

AUSTEN, *Jane (1775—1817)*, English novelist. Wrote six books, *Sense and Sensibility, Pride and Prejudice, Northanger Abbey, Mansfield Park, Emma* and *Persuasion,* which are among the greatest novels in the English language. They have seldom been 'out of print' since they were first published.

BACH, *Johan Sebastian (1685—1750)*. German composer and organist; was one of the founders of his country's tradition of orchestral music. Among his works are the *Mass in B Minor,* the *St. Matthew Passion* and many cantatas and works for the organ.

BACON, *Francis (1561—1626)*. Leading English politician during the reigns of Queen Elizabeth I and King James I, but it is as an author that he is largely remembered. His best-known works are his *Novum Organum* and his *Essays.*

BALZAC, *Honoré de (1799—1850)*. French novelist, famous for his penetrating studies of the society of his time. Among his best-known novels are *Le Père Goriot* and *La Cousine Bette.*

BEETHOVEN, *Ludwig van (1770—1827)*. German composer, famous in particular for his symphonies. By the age of thirty he was nearly deaf, though much of his great music was written after this time.

BERLIOZ, *Hector (1803—1869)*. French composer of symphonies, operas and songs. His best known symphonic work is *Romeo and Juliet.*

BIZET, *Georges (1838—1875)*. French composer of operas, including *The Pearl-Fishers* and *Carmen,* which is one of the world's most popular operas.

BLAKE, *William (1757—1827)*. British poet and artist; author of many religious works, among them the *Prophetic Books* from which the popular hymn 'Jerusalem' is taken.

BOTTICELLI, *Sandro (1444—1510).* Italian Renaissance painter of the Florentine school. His greatest works are in art galleries in Florence.

BRAHMS, *Johannes (1833—1897).* German composer, whose works include several major symphonies, sonatas and much piano music popular with concert audiences.

BRITTEN, *Benjamin (1913—1976)* One of Britain's finest composers, his most famous work is the opera *Peter Grimes.* He had a particular interest in working with children, and was closely associated with the Aldeburgh Festival.

BRONTË, *Sisters: Charlotte (1816—1855), Emily (1818—1848)* and *Anne (1820—1849).* English novelists. Charlotte's books include *Jane Eyre, Shirley* and *Villette;* Emily wrote *Wuthering Heights;* Anne's two books were *Agnes Grey* and *The Tenant of Wildfell Hall.* Of these, *Jane Eyre* and *Wuthering Heights* are the most widely read today.

BROWNING, *Robert (1812—1889).* English poet. Some of his best known works are *Paracelsus, Sordello* and *The Ring and the Book.*

BRUEGHEL, *Pieter, the Elder (1520—1569).* Flemish painter; one of the greatest of his period and founder of a school of artists.

BURNS, *Robert (1759—1796).* Scottish poet, famous for such poems as *Tam o'Shanter* and *The Cotter's Saturday Night* and for such popular songs as *Auld Lang Syne.*

BYRON, *George Gordon, Lord (1788—1824).* English poet, whose work has remained constantly 'in print' for a century and a half. He died in Greece, to which he had gone to aid the Greeks in their struggle for independence.

CÉZANNE, *Paul (1839—1906).* One of the greatest of the French Post-Impressionist painters. Like many of his contemporaries, he was not fully appreciated as an artist during his lifetime.

CHAUCER, *Geoffrey (1340—1400).* One of the greatest of English poets. His *Canterbury Tales* are widely read and enjoyed today.

CHEKHOV, *Anton (1860—1904).* Russian writer of short stories and plays. Among his best-known works are the plays *The Cherry Orchard, The Three Sisters* and *Uncle Vanya.*

CHIPPENDALE, *Thomas (c. 1718—1779).* English furniture designer, who set the pattern for the furnishing of thousands of British households. Surviving examples of his work sell for many hundreds of pounds

CHOPIN, *Frédéric (1810—1849).* Polish composer and musician, famed for his piano compositions. It was a phrase of his music, broadcast over and over again by Warsaw Radio in 1939, which signalled to the world that the Polish Army was still holding out against the invading Germans.

COLERIDGE, *Samuel Taylor (1772—1834).* Poet, philosopher and critic. In the first rank of English poets. Some of his best-known works are *Kubla Khan, The Ancient Mariner* and *Christabel.*

CONFUCIUS *(551—479 B.C.).* The most famous Eastern philosopher, whose collected sayings, called *Confucian Analects,* are often quoted.

CONSTABLE, *John (1776—1837).* British landscape painter whose *Flatford Mill* is one of the best of the rural scenes he painted of his native suffolk.

DANTE ALIGHIERI *(1265—1321).* Italy's greatest poet. He was also a soldier and politician and at one time was sentenced to be burned at the stake for his political allegiance. His greatest work is the *Divina Commedia.*

DEBUSSY, *Claude Achille (1862—1918).* French composer; wrote many well-known piano pieces, including *Clair de Lune.* He was a major influence on 20th c. music.

DEGAS, *(Hilaire, Germain) Edgar (1834—1917).* French Impressionist painter, famous for his studies of ballet dancers.

DICKENS, *Charles (1812—1870).* Leading English novelist, who is still widely read. His best-known works include *David Copperfield, Oliver Twist, The Pickwick Papers, Great Expectations* and *A Christmas Carol.*

DOSTOEVSKY, *Fyodor (1821—1881).* Russian novelist,

140

whose work has had much influence on subsequent writing. Among his best-known novels are *Crime and Punishment, The Idiot* and *The Brothers Karamazov.*

DUMAS, *Alexandre (1802—1870).* French novelist and dramatist. His best-remembered novels are *The Three Musketeers* and *Twenty Years After,* His son Alexandre (1824—1895) was also an author and playwright.

ELGAR, *Sir Edward (1857—1934).* English composer; wrote 'Land of Hope and Glory' as part of the *Pomp and Circumstance* march. His *Enigma Variations* is a popular concert work, and he also wrote the oratorio, *The Dream of Gerontius,* and the symphonic study *Falstaff.*

ELIOT, *Thomas Stearns (1888—1964).* American-born but British-domiciled poet and playwright, whose poems have greatly influenced modern poetry.

EPSTEIN, *Jacob (1880—1959).* Sculptor whose early work was ridiculed, but whose reputation is now high among modern sculptors.

EURIPIDES *(c. 484—407 B.C.).* Greek dramatist, famous for his tragedies, only a few of which survive. Among the best known are *Alcestis, Medea* and *The Trojan Women.*

FLAUBERT, *Gustave (1821—1880).* French author, well known for his novel *Madame Bovary.*

GAUGUIN, *Paul (1848—1903).* French painter, renowned for his pictures of life in the Pacific Islands.

GIOTTO *(1267—1337).* Italian painter, considered the first painter whose work truly belonged to the Renaissance rather than the Middle Ages.

GOETHE, *Johann Wolfgang von (1749—1832).* German poet; the most famous of his works is his play *Faust.* In German writing he takes much the same position as Shakespeare does in the history of English literature and drama. He was also a scientist of considerable importance.

GOGOL, *Nikolai Vasilievich (1809—1852).* Russian novelist and dramatist. His best-known works are his novel *Dead Souls* and his play *The Government Inspector.*

GORKY, *Maxim (1868—1936).* Russian novelist and dramatist. His best-known works are the novels *Mother* and *Comrades,* and the play *The Lower Depths.*

GOYA Y LUCIENTES, *Francisco (1746—1828).* Spanish painter and official Court artist. Although most of his works are in Spain, several paintings can be seen in the National Gallery in London.

GRECO, EL *(1542—1614).* The correct name of this Spanish artist was Domenico Theotocopouli, but his associations with the island of Crete led to the name 'El Greco'. His paintings and sculpture were religious in character.

HANDEL, *George Frederick (1685—1759).* Composer; German-born, but became a British subject. He wrote nearly fifty operas and many oratorios, including *The Messiah.*

HARDY, *Thomas (1840—1928).* English poet and novelist. Among his best-known novels are *Tess of the d'Urbervilles, Far from the Madding Crowd, The Mayor of Casterbridge, The Return of the Native* and *Jude the Obscure.*

HAYDN, *Franz Joseph (1732—1809).* Austrian composer of many symphonies, operas, oratorios and anthems. His oratorios *The Creation* and *The Seasons* are performed frequently.

HOGARTH, *William (1697—1764).* English painter, best remembered for his satirical cartoons of eighteenth-century life and manners in England.

HOLBEIN, *Hans, the Younger (1497—1543).* German portrait painter, several of whose pictures are in the National Gallery in London. His painting of the family of King Henry VII was lost in the Great Fire of London, but much of his work remains.

HOMER *(c. 850 B.C.?).* Probably born in Greece, he was the author of two great works, *The Iliad* and *The Odyssey.*

JOHNSON, *Samuel (1709—1784).* English poet, essayist and lexicographer. Much information regarding him comes to us by way of his biographer, James Boswell.

JONSON, *Ben (1572—1637).* English dramatist, famous for such comedies as *Volpone* and *The Alchemist*.

JOYCE, *James (1882—1941)*. Irish author; spent most of his life in Italy, Switzerland and France. His best-known works are *A Portrait of the Artist as a Young Man, Ulysses* and *Finnegan's Wake*.

KEATS, *John (1795—1821)*. English poet; wrote for only about five years, but his outstanding work had a tremendous influence on later poets. Among his best-remembered writings are *Endymion, The Eve of St Agnes, Ode on a Grecian Urn* and *Ode to a Nightingale*.

LAWRENCE, *David Herbert (1885—1930)*. English novelist and poet; also wrote a number of penetrating travel essays. His leading novels include *Sons and Lovers, Aaron's Rod. The Rainbow* and *Women in Love*.

LEONARDO DA VINCI *(1452—1519)*. Italian painter, sculptor, engineer, botanist, zoologist. Leonardo's greatest achievement was the *Mona Lisa,* perhaps the most famous painting in the world.

LIEBNIZ, *Gottfried (1646—1716)*. German philosopher and mathematician whose main ideas were included in his *Monadology*.

LISZT, *Franz (1811—1886)*. Hungarian pianist and composer. His piano music, including the *Hungarian Rhapsodies,* is often heard at concerts.

MANET, *Édouard (1832—1883)*. French Impressionist painter; was one of the first painters to use colour to express light and shadow.

MARLOWE, *Christopher (1564—1593)*. English dramatist and poet, whose work undoubtedly influenced Shakespeare's early plays. His best-known plays are *Dr Faustus, Tamburlaine* and *The Jew of Malta*.

MARX, *Karl (1818—1883)*. A German philosopher, he was the main founder of communism. His great work *Das Kapital* was published in London.

MATISSE, *Henri (1869—1954)*. French painter. One of the leading artists of the modern schools, he was known especially for his use of pure colour and for his intricate compositions.

MAUPASSANT, *Guy de (1850—1893).* French writer, famous for his short stories.

MELVILLE, *Herman (1819—1891).* American novelist, many of whose writings dealt with the sea. His best-known books are *Moby Dick, Billy Budd* and *Typee.*

MENDELSSOHN-BARTHOLDY, *Jakob Ludwig Felix (1809—1847).* German composer, whose works are often played. Among his best-loved compositions are the oratorio *Elijah,* the '*Scotch*' *Symphony,* the '*Italian*' *Symphony* and the overture *Fingal's Cave.*

MICHELANGELO BUONAROTTI *(1475—1564).* Italian sculptor, architect and painter. The most famous of the Florentine artists, he painted the frescoes in the Sistine Chapel in Rome.

MILL, *John Stuart (1806—1873).* British philosopher and reformer, his most famous work is *On Liberty,* which contains his political views.

MILTON, *John (1608—1674).* One of the greatest English poets. Among his best-known works are *Paradise Lost, Samson Agonistes* and *Areopagitica.*

MOLIÈRE *(Jean Baptiste Poquelin) (1622—1673).* Leading French dramatist. His most popular plays include *Tartuffe, Le Bourgeois gentilhomme* and *L'École des Maris.*

MOORE, *Henry (1898—   ).* One of Britain's and the world's greatest sculptors, Moore is most known for his bulky, rounded reclining figures.

MOZART, *Wolfang Amadeus (1756—1791).* Austrian composer. His most popular works include the operas *The Magic Flute* and *The Marriage of Figaro,* and many symphonies, concerti and string quartets.

NIETSCHE, *Friedrich (1844—1900).* German philosopher who expounded the idea that the real goal of men is to become supermen, and who is sometimes said to have influenced the music of Wagner and the ideas of Nazism.

OVID *(43 B.C.—A.D. 17).* Roman poet; author of the

Heroides, the *Amores,* the *Metamorphoses* and many other works which are read both in Latin and in translation.

PICASSO, *Pablo (1881—1973).* The best-known of modern painters, Picasso in his long career adopted many styles, and founded the Cubist school. His most famous painting is perhaps *Guernica,* which depicts the bombing of the town in the Spanish Civil War.

PROUST, *Marcel (1871—1922).* French novelist, famed for his series of novels *A la Recherche du Temps Perdu.*

PUCCINI, *Giacomo (1858—1924).* Italian composer of many popular operas, including *La Bohème* and *Madame Butterfly.*

PURCELL, *Henry (1658—1695).* English composer. He wrote much fine church music, including chants for psalms, while organist at London's Westminster Abbey.

PUSHKIN, *Alexander (1799—1837).* Russian poet and writer of stories. One of his most famous short stories is *The Queen of Spades.*

RACHMANINOV, *Sergei Vassilievich (1873—1943).* Russian composer and pianist; wrote many popular concert works and also several operas.

RACINE, *Jean (1639—1699).* Leading French tragic dramatist. His best-known plays include *Phèdre* and *Andromaque.*

RAPHAEL, *Sanzio (1483—1520).* One of the greatest Italian painters of the Renaissance. His works are found in art galleries throughout the world.

REMBRANDT, *Harmensz van Rijn (1606—1669).* Dutch artist; one of the world's greatest portrait painters. Some of his work can be seen in London's National Gallery.

RENOIR, *Piere Auguste (1841—1919).* French Impressionist painter, famous in particular for his studies of women. His works appear in galleries all over the world.

REYNOLDS, *Sir Joshua (1723—1792).* The first President of the Royal Academy and the greatest English portrait painter of his day.

RODIN, *Auguste (1840—1917)* French sculptor who began as a stone-mason and ultimately achieved such great work as *The Thinker* and *The Kiss.*

ROSSINI, *Gioacchino Antonio (1793—1868).* Italian operatic composer, best known for *The Barber of Seville* and *William Tell.*

ROUSSEAU, *Jean Jacques (1712—1778).* French writer and philosopher. His best-known writings include *Confessions, Émile* and *Le Contrat Social.*

RUBENS, *Peter Paul (1577—1640).* One of the best known and appreciated of the Flemish school of painters; he had much influence on later artists. His paintings are found in major art galleries all over the world.

RUSSELL, *Bertrand (1872—1970).* British philosopher, logician and mathematician. Always a controversial figure, in a long life he was twice imprisoned for vigorous protests against war and the use of nuclear weapons.

SCHUBERT, *Franz Peter (1797—1828).* Austrian composer; died at the age of thirty-one. His many songs and his chamber music are very popular, as is his *Unfinished Symphony.*

SCHUMANN, *Robert (1810—1856).* German composer, renowned for his symphonies, chamber music and many major piano works.

SCHWEITZER, *Albert (1875—1965).* German philsopher, musician and doctor, he was best known as a missionary who devoted much of his life to his hospital at Lamberéné, in equatorial Africa.

SHAKESPEARE, *William (1564—1616).* English dramatist and poet, generally regarded as the world's greatest playwright. His wide range of tragedies, historical dramas and comedies has been performed more than the work of any other dramatist in history.

SHAW, *George Bernard (1856—1950).* Irish playwright and critic. Among his best-known plays are *Pygmalion, Caesar and Cleopatra, Man and Superman* and *Saint Joan.*

SHELLEY, *Percy Bysshe (1792—1822).* English poet. In his day he was considered revolutionary; today he is regarded as a poetic genius. Among his best-known writings are *Adonais, Prometheus Unbound* and *To a Skylark*.

SIBELIUS, *Jean (1865—1957).* Finnish composer, renowned for his tone-poems, particularly *Finlandia*.

STENDHAL *(Henri Beyle) (1783—1842).* French novelist; author of *Le Rouge et le Noir* and *La Chartreuse de Parme*.

STEVENSON, *Robert Louis (1850—1894).* English novelist and poet, author of *Treasure Island, Kidnapped, The Strange Case of Dr Jekyll and Mr Hyde* and many other widely read books.

STRAUSS, *Johann, the Younger (1825—1899).* Austrian composer. His best-known works include the *Blue Danube Waltz* and *Tales from the Vienna Woods,* and the opera *Die Fledermaus*.

STRAUSS, *Richard (1864—1949).* German composer, best known for such operas as *Der Rosenkavalier* and *Elektra* and such compositions as *Till Eulenspiegel*.

SWIFT, *Jonathan (1667—1745).* English satirist, author of *Gulliver's Travels*.

TCHAIKOWSKY, *Peter Ilyich (1840—1893),* Russian composer of symphonic, operatic and ballet music, including *Swan Lake, Nutcracker Suite* and *The Sleeping Beauty*. Among his most popular works are the *1812 Overture* and the Fifth and Sixth symphonies.

TENNYSON, *Alfred, Lord (1809—1892).* English poet. He was made Poet Laureate for his consistently high standard of work over many years. His greatest verses, such as *The Idylls of the King,* had medieval England as their subject.

TITIAN *(c. 1477—1576).* The greatest painter of the Venetian school. Among his best-known portraits are those of Charles V, and Pope Paul III. His paintings of religious and mythological subjects are particularly brilliant.

TOLSTOY, *Leo Nikolayevich, Count (1828—1910).* Russian novelist, two of whose works, *War and Peace* and *Anna Karenina,* are considered among the greatest novels of all time.

147

TURNER, *Joseph Mallord William (1775—1851).* English painter, famous for his seascapes and landscapes in which he devoted himself to the study of light, using brilliant, luminous colour.

TWAIN, *Mark (Samuel Langhorne Clemens) (1835—1910).* American novelist; author of *Tom Sawyer, Huckleberry Finn, The Prince and the Pauper* and *Pudd'nhead Wilson.*

VAN DYCK, *Sir Anthony (1599—1641).* Flemish portrait painter, appointed Court painter to King Charles I of England.

VAN GOGH, *Vincent (1853—1890).* Dutch painter, who in a short period of seven years as an artist-produced vividly coloured canvases which are known and loved throughout the world.

VELASQUEZ, *Diego Rodriguez de Silva y (1599—1660).* Spanish portrait painter, famous in particular for his Court paintings such as *Las Meninas (The Maids of Honour).* His work influenced the development of modern painting.

VERDI, *Giuseppe (1813—1901).* Italian composer of church and operatic music. He wrote a number of operas which are widely performed, such as *Aida, Rigoletto* and *La Traviata.*

VERMEER, VAN DELFT, *Jan (1632—1675).* Dutch painter of portraits and landscapes, famed for his beautiful studies of light and its effects.

VERONESE, *Paolo (1528—1588).* Italian painter of the Veronese and Venetian Schools. His pictures are remarkable for their colouring.

VIRGIL *(70—19 B.C.).* Considered the greatest of all the Roman poets. His major work is the unfinished *Aeneid,* based on the story of the settlement of Aeneas in Italy after the destruction of Troy.

VOLTAIRE *(François Marie Arouet) (1694—1778).* French writer and satirist. Among his leading works are *Candide* and the *Dictionnaire Philosophique.*

WAGNER, *Richard (1813—1883).* German composer, whose operas, revolutionary in style in their day, include *Die*

Walküre, Lohengrin, Die Meistersinger and *Tristan und Isolde*.

WOOLF, *Virginia (1882—1941)*. English novelist and critic. Among her best-known novels are *Mrs Dalloway, To the Lighthouse* and *The Waves*.

WORDSWORTH, *William (1770—1850)*. English poet, noted for his supreme mastery of language. Was made Poet Laureate in 1843.

WREN, *Sir Christopher (1632—1732)*. English architect-scientist. Was called upon by Charles II to plan repairs to old St Paul's Cathedral, but before these could be carried out the Cathedral was gutted in the Great Fire of London, and his work became that of designing the present Cathedral. He also designed more than fifty other churches.

YEATS, *William Butler (1865—1939)*. Irish poet. One of the great poets of recent times, he was awarded the Nobel Prize for Literature in 1923.

PEOPLE AND SPORT

What is the purpose of sport? Is it records, results or simply the most enjoyable method of keeping healthy? Nobody can give the complete answer, but it is probably a combination of all three.

Every sport has its own story—usually a fascinating history and an origin far back in time. In the following pages you will find brief histories of some of the most popular sports, with their principal facts and figures.

Athletics

The first great athletes were the Greeks, who held Olympic Games more than two thousand seven hundred years ago. These Games were a regular feature of Greek life for more than a thousand years, but when the Romans abolished them, in 394 A.D., athletics became almost a forgotten art for many centuries. It was not until about two hundred years ago that cross-country running for wagers renewed interest in the sport. By the eighteen-fifties most schools and athletic teams and the universities held their own championships. The standards were low, however, compared with those of the present day. It took seventy years to push the high-jump record from six feet to seven feet, and long-distance runners of today have clipped many minutes off the best times ever recorded by their grandfathers.

It was the revival of the Olympic Games in 1896 that made athletics a sport for the millions, for the appeal of international competition is greater than any other.

Here are some of the world's most recent records:

Some of the world record performances for men are listed opposite.

World Records

In 1976 the International Amateur Athletics Federation congress committee decided to recognise world records for events up to and including distances of 400 metres only if the record claimed had been timed electrically. The following list therefore includes only official world records (i.e. electrically timed) for these events. Were hand timing recognised, the records would be 9.9 seconds for 100 metres, 19.8 seconds for 200 metres and 13.1 seconds for the 110 metres hurdles, all by more than one athlete.

Running and Walking Events

Event	Holder	Nation	Record	Year
100 m	J. Hindes	USA	9.95 s	1968
200 m	T. Smith	USA	19.93 s	1968
400 m	L. Evans	USA	43.86 s	1968
800 m	A. Juan-torena	Cuba	1 min. 43.44 s	1977
1,500 m	F. Bayi	Tanzania	3 min. 32.20 s	1974
5,000 m	D. Quax	New Zealand	13 min. 12.90 s	1977
10,000 m	S. Kimambwe	Kenya	27 min. 30.50 s	1977
110 m hurdles	A. Casanas	Cuba	13.21 s	1977
400 m hurdles	E. Moses	USA	47.45 s	1977
3,000 m steeple-chase	A. Garderud	Sweden	8 min. 08.02 s	1976
Marathon	D. Clayton	Australia	2 hr. 08 min. 33.6 s	1969
20 km walk	D. Bautista	Mexico	1 hr. 23 min. 39.8 s	1976

Event	Holder	Nation	Record	Year
50 km walk	V. Soldat-enko	USSR	3 hr. 54 min. 40 s.	1976

Field Events

Event	Holder	Nation	Record	Year
High Jump	V. Yashenko	USSR	2.33 m	1977
Pole Vault	D. Roberts	USA	5.70 m	1976
Long Jump	R. Beamon	USA	8.90 m	1968
Triple Jump	J. de Oliveira	Brazil	17.89 m	1975
Shot	A. Barish-nikov	USSR	22.00 m	1976
Discus	M. Wilkins	USA	70.86 m	1976
Hammer	W. Schmidt	W. Germany	79.30 m	1975
Javelin	M. Nemeth	Hungary	94.58 m	1976
Decathlon	B. Jenner	USA	8618 pts	1976

Olympic Champions

The reigning Olympic champions (1976 games) are as follows:

100 m : H. Crawford (Trinidad and Tobago)
200 m : D. Quarrie (Jamaica)
400 m : A. Juantorena (Cuba)
800 m : A. Juantorena (Cuba)
1,500 m : J. Walker (New Zealand)
5,000 m : L. Viren (Finland)
10,000 m : L. Viren (Finland)
110 m hurdles : G. Drut (France)
400 m hurdles : E. Moses (USA)
3,000 m steeplechase :
A. Garderud (Sweden)
Marathon : W. Cierpinski (E. Germany)
20 km walk : D. Bautista (Mexico)
High jump : J. Wszola (Poland)
Pole Vault : T. Slusarski (Poland)
Long jump : A. Robinson (USA)
Triple jump : V. Saneyev (USSR)

Shot : U. Beyer (E. Germany)
Discus : M. Wilkins (USA)
Hammer : Y. Sedyh (USSR)

Javelin : M. Nemeth (Hungary)
Decathlon : B. Jenner (USA)

Football

The history of football may date as far back as Roman times, when men of the army probably played *harpastum,* a Roman game remarkably like modern Rugby Football. In the sixteenth century the game was played in England by whole villages, often with as many as a hundred men on each side. Injuries were numerous and severe, and the game was extremely dangerous until the early part of the last century when many schools in England improved it and set up codes of rules. These became standardised in the eighteen-sixties, when those who favoured 'the handling game' formed the Rugby Union and those who preferred non-handling established the Football Association. There are now seven distinct forms of football, but the three most widely played are Association (eleven players, world wide), Rugby Union (fifteen players; principally Britain, France, Australia, New Zealand, South Africa) and Rugby League (thirteen players; Britain, France, Australia, New Zealand).

Association Football

The world record crowd at an Association Football match was 200,000 at the World Cup Final of 1950, between Brazil and Uruguay in Rio de Janeiro. The highest score in a match recognised as official was Arbroath 36, Bon Accord 0, in a Scottish Cup match in 1885. The highest score in an international match was England 17, Australia 0, at Sydney in 1951.

World Cup Winners

1930 Uruguay	1958 Brazil
1934 Italy	1962 Brazil
1938 Italy	1966 England
1950 Uruguay	1970 Brazil
1954 West Germany	1974 West Germany

F. A. Cup Winners

1873–4	Oxford University	1888–9	Preston N.E.
1874–5	Royal Engineers	1889–90	Blackburn Rovers
1875–6	Wanderers	1890–1	Blackburn Rovers
1876–7	Wanderers	1891–2	West Bromwich Albion
1877–8	Wanderers		
1878–9	Old Etonians	1892–3	Wolverhampton Wanderers
1879–80	Clapham Rovers		
1880–1	Old Carthusians	1893–4	Notts County
1881–2	Old Etonians	1894–5	Aston Villa
1882–3	Blackburn Olympic	1895–6	Sheffield Wednesday
1883–4	Blackburn Rovers	1896–7	Aston Villa
1884–5	Blackburn Rovers	1897–8	Nottingham Forest
1885–6	Blackburn Rovers	1898–9	Sheffield United
		1899–1900	Bury
1886–7	Aston Villa	1900–1	Tottenham H.
1887–8	West Bromwich Albion	1901–2	Sheffield United
		1902–3	Bury

1903–4	Manchester City	1935–6	Arsenal
1904–5	Aston Villa	1936–7	Sunderland
1905–6	Everton	1937–8	Preston N.E.
1906–7	Sheffield Wednesday	1938–9	Portsmouth
		1939–45	*No competition*
1907–8	Wolverhampton Wanderers	1945–6	Derby County
		1946–7	Charlton Athletic
1908–9	Manchester United	1947–8	Manchester United
1909–10	Newcastle United	1948–9	Wolverhampton Wanderers
1910–11	Bradford City		
1911–12	Barnsley	1949–50	Arsenal
1912–13	Aston Villa	1950–1	Newcastle United
1913–14	Burnley	1951–2	Newcastle United
1914–15	Sheffield United	1952–3	Blackpool
1915–19	*No competition*	1953–4	West Bromwich Albion
1919–20	Aston Villa		
1920–1	Tottenham H.	1954–5	Newcastle United
1921–2	Huddersfield T.	1955–6	Manchester City
1922–3	Bolton Wanderers	1956–7	Aston Villa
		1957–8	Bolton Wanderers
1923–4	Newcastle United	1958–9	Nottingham Forest
1924–5	Sheffield United		
1925–6	Bolton Wanderers	1959–60	Wolverhampton Wanderers
1926–7	Cardiff City	1960–1	Tottenham H.
1927–8	Blackburn Rovers	1961–2	Tottenham H.
1928–9	Bolton Wanderers	1962–3	Manchester United
1929–30	Arsenal	1963–4	West Ham United
1930–1	West Bromwich Albion		
		1964–5	Liverpool
1931–2	Newcastle United	1965–6	Everton
1932–3	Everton	1966–7	Tottenham H.
1933–4	Manchester City	1967–8	West Bromwich A.
1934–5	Sheffield Wednesday	1968–9	Manchester City
		1969–70	Chelsea

1970–1 Arsenal
1971–2 Leeds United
1972–3 Sunderland

1973–4 Liverpool
1974–5 West Ham United
1975–6 Southampton
1976–7 Manchester United

Football League Champions (1st Division)

1890–1 Everton
1891–2 Sunderland
1892–3 Sunderland
1893–4 Aston Villa
1894–5 Sunderland
1895–6 Aston Villa
1896–7 Aston Villa
1897–8 Sheffield United
1898–9 Aston Villa
1899–1900
      Aston Villa
1900–1 Liverpool
1901–2 Sunderland
1902–3 Shefield Wed.
1903–4 Sheffield
      Wednesday
1904–5 Newcastle United
1905–6 Liverpool
1906–7 Newcastle United
1907–8 Manchester United
1908–9 Newcastle United
1909–10 Aston Villa
1910–11 Manchester United
1911–12 Blackburn Rovers
1912–13 Sunderland
1913–14 Blackburn Rovers
1914–15 Everton
1915–19 *No competition*
1919–20 West Bromwich
      Albion

1920–1 Burnley
1921–2 Liverpool
1922–3 Liverpool
1923–4 Huddersfield
      Town
1924–5 Huddersfield
      Town
1925–6 Huddersfield Town
1926–7 Newcastle United
1927–8 Everton
1928–9 Sheffield
      Wednesday
1929–30 Sheffield
      Wednesday
1930–1 Arsenal
1931–2 Everton
1932–3 Arsenal
1933–4 Arsenal
1934–5 Arsenal
1935–6 Sunderland
1936–7 Manchester City
1937–8 Arsenal
1938–9 Everton
1939–46 *No competition*
1946–7 Liverpool
1947–8 Arsenal
1948–9 Portsmouth
1949–50 Portsmouth
1950–1 Tottenham
      Hotspur

156

1951–2	Manchester United	1961–2	Ipswich
1952–3	Arsenal	1962–3	Everton
1953–4	Wolverhampton Wanderers	1963–4	Liverpool
		1964–5	Manchester United
1954–5	Chelsea	1965–6	Liverpool
1955–6	Manchester United	1966–7	Manchester United
		1967–8	Manchester City
1956–7	Manchester United	1968–9	Leeds
		1969–70	Everton
1957–8	Wolverhampton Wanderers	1970–1	Arsenal
		1971–2	Derby County
1958–9	Wolverhampton Wanderers	1972–3	Liverpool
		1973–4	Leeds United
1959–60	Burnley	1974–5	Derby County
1960–1	Tottenham H.	1975 6	Liverpool
		1976–7	Liverpool

Scottish Cup Winners

1875–6	Queen's Park	1894–5	St Bernard's
1876–7	Vale of Leven	1895–6	Hearts
1877–8	Vale of Leven	1896–7	Rangers
1878–9	Vale of Leven	1897–8	Rangers
1879–80	Queen's Park	1898–9	Celtic
1880–1	Queen's Park	1899–1900	Celtic
1881–2	Queen's Park	1900–1	Hearts
1882–3	Dumbarton	1901–2	Hibernian
1883–4	Queen's Park	1902–3	Rangers
1884–5	Renton	1903–4	Celtic
1885–6	Queen's Park	1904–5	Third Lanark
1886–7	Hibernian	1905–6	Hearts
1887–8	Renton	1906–7	Celtic
1888–9	Third Lanark	1907–8	Celtic
1889–90	Queen's Park	1908–9	*Cup withheld (riot)*
1890–1	Hearts	1909–10	Dundee
1891–2	Celtic	1910–11	Celtic
1892–3	Queen's Park	1911–12	Celtic
1893–4	Rangers	1912–13	Falkirk

1913–14 Celtic	1950–1 Celtic
1914–19 *No competition*	1951–2 Motherwell
1919–20 Kilmarnock	1952–3 Rangers
1920–1 Patrick Thistle	1953–4 Celtic
1921–2 Morton	1954–5 Clyde
1922–3 Celtic	1955–6 Hearts
1923–4 Airdrieonians	1956–7 Falkirk
1924–5 Celtic	1957–8 Clyde
1925–6 St Mirren	1958–9 St. Mirren
1926–7 Celtic	1959–60 Rangers
1927–8 Rangers	1960–1 Dunfermline
1928–9 Kilmarnock	1961–2 Rangers
1929–30 Rangers	1962–3 Rangers
1930–1 Celtic	1963–4 Rangers
1931–2 Rangers	1964–5 Celtic
1932–3 Celtic	1965–6 Rangers
1933–4 Rangers	1966–7 Celtic
1934–5 Rangers	1967–8 Dunfermline
1935–6 Rangers	1968–9 Celtic
1936–7 Celtic	1969–70 Aberdeen
1937–8 East Fife	1970–1 Celtic
1938–9 Clyde	1971–2 Celtic
1939–46 *No competition*	1972–3 Rangers
1946–7 Aberdeen	1973–4 Celtic
1947–8 Rangers	1974–5 Celtic
1948–9 Rangers	1975–6 Rangers
1949–50 Rangers	1976–7 Celtic

Scottish League Champions

1891–2 Dumbarton	1899–1900 Rangers
1892–3 Celtic	1900–1 Rangers
1893–4 Celtic	1901–2 Rangers]
1894–5 Hearts	1902–3 Hibernian
1895–6 Celtic	1903–4 Third Lanark
1896–7 Hearts	1904–5 Celtic
1897–8 Celtic	1905–6 Celtic
1898–9 Rangers	1906–7 Celtic

1907–8	Celtic	1939–46	*No competition*
1908–9	Celtic	1946–7	Rangers
1909–10	Celtic	**1947–8**	Hibernian
1910–11	Rangers	1948–9	Rangers
1911–12	Rangers	1949–50	Rangers
1912–13	Rangers	1950–1	Hibernian
1913–14	Celtic	1951–2	Hibernian
1914–15	Celtic	1952–3	Rangers
1915–16	Celtic	1953–4	Celtic
1916–17	Celtic	1954–5	Aberdeen
1917–18	Rangers	1955–6	Rangers
1918–19	Celtic	1956–7	Rangers
1919–20	Rangers	1957–8	Hearts
1920–1	Rangers	1958–9	Rangers
1921–2	Celtic	1959–60	Hearts
1922–3	Rangers	1960–1	Rangers
1923–4	Rangers	1961–2	Dundee
1924–**5**	Rangers	1962–3	Rangers
1925–6	Celtic	1963–4	Rangers
1926–7	Rangers	1964–5	Kilmarnock
1927–8	Rangers	1965–6	Celtic
1928–9	Rangers	1966–7	Celtic
1929–30	Rangers	1967–8	Celtic
1930–1	Rangers	1968–9	Celtic
1931–2	Motherwell	1969–70	Celtic
1932–3	Rangers	1970–1	Celtic
1933–4	Rangers	1971–2	Celtic
1934–5	Rangers	1972–3	Celtic
1935–6	Celtic	1973–4	Celtic
1936–7	Rangers	1974–5	Rangers
1937–8	Celtic	1975–6	Rangers
1938–9	Rangers	1976–7	Celtic

Home International Championship (since 1946)

1946–7	England	1949–50	England
1947–8	England	1950–1	Scotland
1948–9	Scotland	1951–2	Wales-England

1952–3	England-Scotland	1964–5	England
1953–4	England	1965–6	England
1954–5	England	1966–7	Scotland
1955–6	England, Scotland, Wales and Ireland	1967–8	England
		1968–9	England
1956–7	England	1969–70	England, Scotland and Wales
1957–8	England-Ireland		
1958–9	England-Ireland	1970–1	England
1959–60	England, Wales and Scotland	1971–2	England and Scotland
1960–1	England	1972–3	England
1961–2	Scotland	1973–4	England and Scotland
1962–3	Scotland		
1963–4	England, Scotland and Ireland	1974–5	England
		1975–6	Scotland
		1976–7	Scotland

Rugby Union
International Championship (since 1946)

1946–7	Wales and England	1961–2	France
1947–8	Ireland	1962–3	England
1948–9	Ireland	1963–4	Scotland and Wales
1949–50	Wales	1964–5	Wales
1950–1	Ireland	1965–6	Wales
1951–2	Wales	1966–7	France
1952–3	England	1967–8	France
1953–4	England, France and Wales	1968–9	Wales
		1969–70	France
1954–5	Wales and France	1970–1	Wales
1955–6	Wales	1971–2	Wales
1956–7	England	1972–3	All five countries finished level
1957–8	England		
1958–9	France	1973–4	Ireland
1959–60	England and France	1974–5	Wales
		1975–6	Wales
1960–1	France	1976–7	France

160

Rugby League
Challenge Cup Winners (since 1946)

1946–7	Bradford Northern	1961–2	Wakefield Trinity
1947–8	Wigan	1962–3	Wakefield Trinity
1948–9	Bradford Northern	1963–4	Widnes
1949–50	Warrington	1964–5	Wigan
1950–1	Wigan	1965–6	St. Helens
1951–2	Workington Town	1966–7	Featherstone Rovers
1952–3	Huddersfied	1967–8	Leeds
1953–4	Warrington	1968–9	Castleford
1954–5	Barrow	1969–70	Castleford
1955–6	St. Helens	1970–1	Leigh
1956–7	Leeds	1971–2	St. Helens
1957–8	Wigan	1972–3	Featherstone Rovers
1958–9	Wigan	1973–4	Warrington
1959–60	Wakefield Trinity	1974–5	Widnes
1960–1	St. Helens	1975–6	St. Helens
		1976–7	Leeds

Golf

Golf was begun in Scotland about five hundred years ago and shares with Association Football the distinction of being a truly international game, golf courses now being everywhere.

British Open Championship Winners (since 1948)

1948	T. H. Cotton (Great Britain)	1955	P. W. Thomson
		1956	P. W. Thomson
1949	A. D. Locke (South Africa)	1957	A. D. Locke
		1958	P. W. Thomson
1950	A. D. Locke	1959	G. J. Player (South Africa)
1951	M. Faulkner (unattached)		
		1960	K. Nagle (Australia)
1952	A. D. Locke	1961	A. Palmer (U.S.A.)
1953	B. Hogan (U.S.A.)	1962	A. Palmer
1954	P. W. Thomson (Australia)	1963	R. J. Charles (New Zealand)

1964	A. Lema (U.S.A.)	1970	J. Nicklaus (U.S.A.)
1965	P. W. Thomson	1971	L. Trevino (Mexico)
1966	J. W. Nicklaus (U.S.A.)	1972	L. Trevino
		1973	T. Weiskopf (U.S.A.)
1967	R. de Vicenzo (Argentina)	1974	G. J. Player (South Africa)
1968	G. J. Player (South Africa)	1975	T. Watson (U.S.A.)
		1976	J. Miller (U.S.A.)
1969	A. Jacklin (Great Britain)	1977	T. Watson (U.S.A.)

Ryder Cup Competition (since 1947)

1963 U.S.A. 23 matches—Great Britain 9 matches
1965 U.S.A. 19½ matches—Great Britain 12½ matches
1967 U.S.A. 23½ matches—Great Britain 8½ matches
1969 Drawn—16 matches each
1971 U.S.A. 18½ matches—Great Britain 13½ matches
1973 U.S.A. 19 matches—Great Britain 13 matches
1975 U.S.A. 21 matches—Great Britain 11 matches
1947 U.S.A. 11 matches—Great Britain 1 match
1949 U.S.A. 7 matches—Great Britain 5 matches
1951 U.S.A. 9½ matches—Great Britain 2½ matches
1953 U.S.A. 6½ matches—Great Britain 5½ matches
1955 U.S.A. 8 matches—Great Britain 4 matches
1957 Great Britain 7½ matches—U.S.A. 4½ matches
1959 U.S.A. 8½ matches—Great Britain 3½ matches
1961 U.S.A. 13 matches—Great Britain 8 matches
1977 U.S.A. 12½ matches—Great Britain 7½ matches

Walker Cup Competition (Amateur) (since 1947)

1947 U.S.A. 8 matches—Great Britain 4 matches
1949 U.S.A. 10 matches—Great Britain 2 matches
1951 U.S.A. 7½ matches—Great Britain 4½ matches
1953 U.S.A. 9 matches—Great Britain 3 matches
1955 U.S.A. 10 matches—Great Britain 2 matches
1957 U.S.A. 8½ matches—Great Britain 3½ matches
1959 U.S.A. 9 matches—Great Britain 3 matches
1961 U.S.A. 11 matches—Great Britain 1 match

1963 U.S.A. 12 matches—Great Britain 8 matches
1965 Drawn—12 matches each
1967 U.S.A. 15 matches—Great Britain 9 matches
1969 U.S.A. 13 matches—Great Britain 11 matches
1971 Great Britain 13 matches—U.S.A. 11 matches
1973 U.S.A. 14 matches—Great Britain 10 matches
1975 U.S.A. 15½ matches—Great Britain 5½ matches
1977 U.S.A. 16 matches—Great Britain 8 matches

Lawn Tennis

This is a modern game born of one much older. Real, or Royal, Tennis was played centuries ago and is still played to a limited extent today, but it is an expensive game.

Wimbledon Champions (Men's Singles)

1879–80	J. T. Hartley	1925	R. Lacoste
1881–6	W. Renshaw	1926	J. Borotra
1887	H. F. Lawford	1927	H. Cochet
1888	E. Renshaw	1928	R. Lacoste
1889	W. Renshaw	1929	H. Cochet
1890	W. J. Hamilton	1930	W. T. Tilden
1891–2	W. Baddeley	1931	S. B. Wood
1893–4	J. Pim	1932	H. E. Vines, Jr.
1895	W. Baddeley	1933	J. H. Crawford
1896	H. S. Mahony	1934–6	F. J. Perry
1897–1900	R. E. Doherty	1937–8	J. D. Budge
1901	A. W. Gore	1939	R. L. Riggs
1902–6	H. L. Doherty	1940–5	*No competition*
1907	N. E. Brookes	1946	Y. Petra
1908–9	A. W. Gore	1947	J. A. Kramer
1910–13	A. F. Wilding	1948	R. Falkenburg
1914	N. E. Brookes	1949	F. Schroeder, Jr.
1915–18	*No competition*	1950	J. E. Patty
1919	G. L. Patterson	1951	R. Savitt
1920–1	W. L. Tilden	1952	F. A. Sedgman
1922	G. L. Patterson	1953	E. V. Seixas
1923	W. M. Johnston	1954	J. Drobný
1924	J. Borotra	1955	M. A. Trabert

163

1956–7	L. A. Hoad	1967	J. D. Newcombe
1958	A. J. Cooper	1968	R. Laver
1959	A. Olmedo	1969	R. Laver
1960	N. A. Fraser	1970	J. D. Newcombe
1961	R. Laver	1971	J. D. Newcombe
1962	R. Laver	1972	S. Smith
1963	C. R. McKinley	1973	J. Kodeš
1964	R. Emerson	1974	J. Connors
1965	R. Emerson	1975	A. Ashe
1966	M. Santana	1976	B. Borg
		1977	B. Borg

Davis Cup (Lawn Tennis Championship)

1947	U.S.A.	4,	Australia	1
1948	U.S.A.	5,	Australia	0
1949	U.S.A.	4,	Australia	1
1950	Australia	4,	U.S.A.	1
1951	Australia	3,	U.S.A.	2
1952	Australia	4,	U.S.A.	1
1953	Australia	4,	U.S.A.	2
1954	U.S.A.	3,	Australia	2
1955	Australia	5,	U.S.A.	0
1956	Australia	5,	U.S.A.	0
1957	Australia	3,	U.S.A.	2
1958	U.S.A.	3,	Australia	2
1959	Australia	3,	U.S.A.	2
1960	Australia	4,	Italy	1
1961	Australia	5,	Italy	0
1962	Australia	5,	Mexico	0
1963	U.S.A.	3,	Australia	2
1964	Australia	3,	U.S.A.	2
1965	Australia	4,	Spain	1
1966	Australia	4,	India	1
1967	Australia	4,	Spain	1
1968	U.S.A.	4,	Australia	1
1969	U.S.A.	5,	Romania	0
1970	U.S.A.	5,	G.F.D.	0
1971	U.S.A.	3,	Romania	2

1972 U.S.A.	3,	Romania	2
1973 Australia	5,	U.S.A.	0
1974 South Africa		(India Scratched)	
1975 Sweden 3		Czechoslovakia 2	
1976 Italy 4		Chile 1	
1977 Australia 3		Italy 1	

Yachting

Probably the most famous yachting event is the series of races for the America's Cup, first competed for in 1851. America has won every contest. Results since 1920:

1920 *Resolute* beat *Shamrock IV*
1930 *Enterprise* beat *Shamrock V*
1934 *Rainbow* beat *Endeavour*
1937 *Ranger* beat *Endeavour II*
1958 *Columbia* beat *Sceptre*
1962 *Weatherly* beat *Gretel*
1964 *Constellation* beat *Sovereign*
1967 *Intrepid* beat *Dame Pattie*
1970 *Intrepid* beat *Dame Pattie*
1977 *Courageous* beat *Australia*

Cricket

Cricket became widespread in England in the seventeenth and eighteenth centuries, then became popular abroad as English settlers went to Australia, New Zealand, South Africa, India, Pakistan and the West Indies, all of which today, except South Africa, play Test Matches. Other countries where cricket is played are Holland, the United States, Canada, South America and most British Colonies, though in none of these does the standard approach what is recognised as 'first class'—the standard of the main national competitions in the Test-playing countries.

The first major overseas tour by an English team was a visit to Australia in 1861—2. It was in Melbourne, in 1877, that Australia won the first of all Test Matches.

Records in Cricket

Some of the most interesting cricket records are the following:

Highest score in first-class cricket—499 not out (Hanif Mohammed, in Pakistan, 1959)

Highest score in Test cricket—365 not out (G. Sobers, West Indies, against Pakistan, in Kingston, 1958)

Highest known score in School cricket—628 not out (A.E. Collins, in a match at Clifton College, Bristol, 1899)

Greatest number of runs in first-class cricket—61,237 between 1905 and 1934 (Sir J. B. Hobbs)

Most runs scored off a six-ball over—36 (G. Sobers of Nottinghamshire, off M. Nash of Glamorgan, at Swansea, 1968)

Highest batting partnership—577 (V. S. Hazare and Gul Mahomed, in Indian cricket, 1947)

Highest score in a season—3,816 (D.C.S. Compton, in 1947, with an average of 90.85)

Greatest number of wickets by a bowler in one match—19 (J.C. Laker, for England against Australia, at Old Trafford, 1956, for 90 runs)

Greatest number of wickets in first-class cricket—4,187 between 1898 and 1930 (W. R. Rhodes)

Greatest total—1,107 (by Victoria against New South Wales, 1926)

Test Matches—England—Australia (The Ashes)

1876–7	Australia 1, England 1
1878–9	Australia 1
1880	England 1
1881–2	Australia 2, drawn 2
1882	Australia 1
1882–3	Australia 2, England 2
1884	England 1, drawn 2
1884–5	England 3, Australia 2
1886	England 3
1886–7	England 2
1887–8	England 1
1888	England 2, Australia 1

1890	England 2, abandoned 1
1891–2	Australia 2, England 1
1893	England 1, drawn 2
1894–5	England 3, Australia 2
1896	England 2, Australia 1
1897–8	Australia 4, England 1
1899	Australia 1, drawn 4
1901–2	Australia 4, England 1
1902	Australia 2, England 1, drawn 2
1903–4	England 3, Australia 2
1905	England 2, drawn 3
1907–8	Australia 4, England 1
1909	Australia 2, England 1, drawn 2
1911–12	England 4, Australia 1
1912	England 1, drawn 2
1920–1	Australia 5
1921	Australia 3, drawn 2
1924–5	Australia 4, England 1
1926	England 1, drawn 4
1928–9	England 4, Australia 1
1930	Australia 2, England 1, drawn 2
1932–3	England 4, Australia 1
1934	Australia 2, England 1, drawn 2
1936–7	Australia 3, England 2
1938	England 1, Australia 1, drawn 2, abandoned 1
1946–7	Australia 3, drawn 2
1948	Australia 4, drawn 1
1950–1	Australia 4, England 1
1953	England 1, drawn 4
1954–5	England 3, Australia 1, drawn 1
1956	England 2, Australia 1, drawn 2
1958–9	Australia 4, drawn 1
1961	Australia 3, England 1, drawn 1
1962–3	Australia 1, England 1, drawn 3
1964	Australia 1, drawn 4
1965–6	Australia 1, England 1, drawn 3

1968	Australia 1, England 1, drawn 3		
1970-1	England 1, drawn 4		
1972	England 2, Australia 2, drawn 1		
1974-5	Australia 4, England 1, drawn 1		
1975	Australia 1, drawn 3		
1977	England 3, drawn 2		

English County Championship

1873	Gloucestershire and Nottinghamshire	1900	Yorkshire
1874	Derbyshire	1901	Yorkshire
1875	Nottinghamshire, Lancashire and Sussex	1902	Yorkshire
		1903	Middlesex
1876	Gloucestershire	1904	Lancashire
1877	Gloucestershire	1905	Yorkshire
1878	Middlesex	1906	Kent
1879	Notts and Lancs	1907	Nottinghamshire
1880	Nottinghamshire	1908	Yorkshire
1881	Lancashire	1909	Kent
1882	Notts and Lancs	1910	Kent
1883	Nottinghamshire	1911	Warwickshire
1884	Nottinghamshire	1912	Yorkshire
1885	Nottinghamshire	1913	Kent
1886	Nottinghamshire	1914	Surrey
1887	Surrey	1919	Yorkshire
1888	Surrey	1920	Middlesex
1889	Surrey, Lancashire and Nottinghamshire	1921	Middlesex
		1922	Yorkshire
1890	Surrey	1923	Yorkshire
1891	Surrey	1924	Yorkshire
1892	Surrey	1925	Yorkshire
1893	Yorkshire	1926	Lancashire
1894	Surrey	1927	Lancashire
1895	Surrey	1928	Lancashire
1896	Yorkshire	1929	Nottinghamshire
1897	Lancashire	1930	Lancashire
1898	Yorkshire	1931	Yorkshire
1899	Surrey	1932	Yorkshire
		1933	Yorkshire

168

1935	Yorkshire	1958	Surrey
1936	Derbyshire	1959	Yorkshire
1937	Yorkshire	1960	Yorkshire
1938	Yorkshire	1961	Hampshire
1939	Yorkshire	1962	Yorkshire
1940-5	No Matches	1963	Yorkshire
1946	Yorkshire	1964	Worcestershire
1947	Middlesex	1965	Worcestershire
1948	Glamorgan	1966	Yorkshire
1949	Middlesex and Yorkshire	1967	Yorkshire
		1968	Yorkshire
1950	Lancashire and Surrey	1969	Glamorgan
1951	Warwickshire	1970	Kent
1952	Surrey	1971	Surrey
1953	Surrey	1972	Warwickshire
1954	Surrey	1973	Hampshire
1955	Surrey	1974	Worcestershire
1956	Surrey	1975	Leicestershire
1957	Surrey	1976	Middlesex
		1977	Middlesex and Kent

Gillette Cup Winners

1963	Sussex	1975	Lancashire
1964	Sussex	1976	Northamptonshire
1965	Yorkshire	1977	Middlesex
1966	Warwickshire		
1967	Kent		
1968	Warwickshire		
1969	Yorkshire		
1970	Lancashire		
1971	Lancashire		
1972	Lancashire		
1973	Gloucestershire		
1974	Kent		

Rowing

There is no official world championship, but the events at Henley Royal Regatta in Britain are generally recognised

169

as indicating the champions. The two events which attract most interest are the Grand Challenge Cup and the Diamond Challenge Sculls.

Grand Challenge Cup (for Eights) (since 1949)

Year	Winner	Year	Winner
1949	Leander Club		Viljnius (U.S.S.R.)
1950	Harvard Univ. (U.S.A.)	1965	Ratzerburger Ruderclub (W. Germany)
1951	Lady Margaret B. C. Cambridge	1966	T.S.C. Berlin
1952	Leander Club	1967	S.C. Wissenschaft (E. Germany)
1953	Leander Club	1968	London Univ.
1954	Krylia Sovetov Club (U.S.S.R.)	1969	S. C. Einheit Dreseden (E. Germany)
1955	Univ. of Pennsylvania (U.S.A.)	1970	A.S.K. Vorwarts Rostock (E. Germany)
1956	French Army	1971	Tideway Scullers (Britain)
1957	Cornell Univ. (U.S.A.)		
1958	Trud Club (U.S.S.R.)	1972	W.M.E. Moscow (U.S.S.R.)
1959	Harvard Univ. (U.S.A.)		
1960	Molesey R. C.	1973	TrudKolomna(U.S.S.R.)
1961	U.S.S.R. Navy	1974	TrudKolomna(U.S.S.R.)
1962	Central Sport Club (U.S.S.R.)	1975	Leander/Thames Tradesmen
1963	London Univ.	1976	Thames Tradesmen
1964	Club Zjalghivis	1977	Washington Univ.

Diamond Challenge Sculls (for Single Oarsmen)

Year	Winner	Year	Winner
1950	A. D. Rowe (Leander Club)	1953	T. A. Fox (London R. C.)
1951	T. A. Fox (Pembroke Coll. Camb.)	1954	P. Vlasic (Yugoslavia)
1952	M. T. Wood (Australia)	1955	T. Kocerka (Poland)
		1956	T. Kocerka (Poland)

1957	S. A. Mackenzie (Australia)	1968	H. E. A. Wardell-Yerburgh (Eton Vikings)
1958	S. A. Mackenzie (Australia)		
1959	S. A. Mackenzie (Australia)	1969	H. J. Bohmer (West Germany)
1960	S. A. Mackenzie (Australia)	1970	J. Meissner (West Germany)
1961	S. A. Mackenzie (Australia)	1971	A. Demeddi (Argentine)
1962	S. A. Mackenzie (Australia)	1972	A. Timoschinin
1963	G. Kuttmann (Switzerland)	1973	S. Drea (Eire)
1964	S. Cromwell (U.S.A.)	1974	S. Drea (Eire)
1965	D. M. Spero (U.S.A.)	1975	S. Drea (Eire)
1966	A. Hill (Germany)	1976	E. Hale (Australia)
1967	M. Studach (Switzerland)	1977	T. J. Crooks (Leander Club)

Oxford and Cambridge Boat Race (Putney to Mortlake)

1829	Oxford	1857	Oxford
1836	Cambridge	1858	Cambridge
1839	Cambridge	1859	Oxford
1840	Cambridge	1860	Cambridge
1841	Cambridge	1861	Oxford
1842	Oxford	1862	Oxford
1845	Cambridge	1863	Oxford
1846	Cambridge	1864	Oxford
1849	Cambridge	1865	Oxford
1849	Oxford	1866	Oxford
1852	Oxford	1867	Oxford
1854	Oxford	1868	Oxford
1856	Cambridge	1869	Oxford

1870	Cambridge	1906	Cambridge
1871	Cambridge	1907	Cambridge
1872	Cambridge	1908	Cambridge
1873	Cambridge	1909	Oxford
1874	Cambridge	1910	Oxford
1875	Oxford	1911	Oxford
1876	Cambridge	1912	Oxford
1877	Drawn	1913	Oxford
1878	Oxford	1914	Cambridge
1879	Cambridge	1915–19	*No contest*
1880	Oxford	1920	Cambridge
1881	Oxford	1921	Cambridge
1882	Oxford	1922	Cambridge
1883	Oxford	1923	Oxford
1884	Cambridge	1924	Cambridge
1885	Oxford	1925	Cambridge
1886	Cambridge	1926	Cambridge
1887	Cambridge	1927	Cambridge
1888	Cambridge	1928	Cambridge
1889	Cambridge	1929	Cambridge
1890	Oxford	1930	Cambridge
1891	Oxford	1931	Cambridge
1892	Oxford	1932	Cambridge
1893	Oxford	1933	Cambridge
1894	Oxford	1934	Cambridge
1895	Oxford	1935	Cambridge
1896	Oxford	1936	Cambridge
1897	Oxford	1937	Oxford
1898	Oxford	1938	Oxford
1899	Cambridge	1939	Cambridge
1900	Cambridge	1940–45	*No contest*
1901	Oxford	1946	Oxford
1902	Cambridge	1947	Cambridge
1903	Cambridge	1948	Cambridge
1904	Cambridge	1949	Cambridge
1905	Oxford	1950	Cambridge

172

1951	Cambridge	1964	Cambridge
1952	Oxford	1965	Oxford
1953	Cambridge	1966	Oxford
1954	Oxford	1967	Oxford
1955	Cambridge	1968	Cambridge
1956	Cambridge	1969	Cambridge
1957	Cambridge	1970	Cambridge
1958	Cambridge	1971	Cambridge
1959	Oxford	1972	Cambridge
1960	Oxford	1973	Cambridge
1961	Cambridge	1974	Oxford
1962	Cambridge	1975	Cambridge
1963	Oxford	1976	Oxford
		1977	Oxford

Cross Country
International Championship (since 1946)

1946 France	1957 Belgium	1968 England
1947 France	1958 England	1969 England
1948 Belgium	1959 England	1970 England
1949 France	1960 England	1971 England
1950 France	1961 Belgium	1972 England
1951 England	1962 England	1973 Belgium
1952 France	1963 Belgium	1974 Belgium
1953 England	1964 England	1975 New Zealand
1954 England	1965 England	1976 England
1955 England	1966 England	1977 Belgium
1956 France	1967 England	

Swimming

Standards of swimming have improved very rapidly during the last hundred years as new stokes have been discovered. The 'marathon' in swimming is the Channel swim. This was first achieved in 1874 by Captain M. Webb (Britain), in 21 hours and 45 minutes; in 1950, a time of 10 hours and 50 minutes by Hassan Abdel Rehim (Egypt) was recorded.

World Records

Distance Holder Freestyle		Nation	Time
100 m	J. Skinner	South Africa	49.44 s
200 m	B. Furniss	U.S.A.	1 min. 50.29 s
400 m	B. Goodell	U.S.A.	3 min. 51.56 s
1,500 m	B. Goodell	U.S.A.	15 min. 02.40 s

Backstroke

100 m	J. Naber	U.S.A.	55.49 s
200 m	J. Naber	U.S.A.	1 min. 59.19 s

Breast stroke

100 m	J. Hencken	U.S.A.	1 min. 03.11 s
200 m	D. Wilkie	Gt. Britain	2 min. 15.11 s

Butterfly

100 m	M. Spitz	U.S.A.	54.27 s
200 m	M. Bruner	U.S.A.	1 min. 59.23 s

Table Tennis

This table-top version of Lawn Tennis is played in almost every country of the world, and in Asia and Central Europe it has become one of the major sports.

Organised table tennis came in 1927, with the formation of the English Table Tennis Association.

World Championships

Men's Singles

1950–51	J. Leach (England)
1951–52	H. Satoh (Japan)
1952–53	F. Sido (Hungary)
1953–54	I. Ogimura (Japan)
1954–55	T. Tanaka (Japan)
1955–56	I. Ogimura (Japan)

174

1956–57	T. Tanaka (Japan)
1958–59	Jung Kuo-Tuan (China)
1960–61	Chuang Tse-tung (China)
1962–63	Chuang Tse-tung (China)
1964–65	Chuang Tse-Tung (China)
1966–67	N. Hasegawa (Japan)
1968–69	F. Itoh (Japan)
1970–71	S. Bengtsson (Sweden)
1972–73	Hsi En-Ting (China)
1974–75	I. Jonyer (Hungary)
1976–77	S. Gomozkov (U.S.S.R.)

Swaythling Cup (Men's Championship)

1950–51	Czechoslovakia
1951–52	Hungary
1952–53	England
1953–54	Japan
1954–55	Japan
1955–56	Japan
1956–57	Japan
1958–59	Japan
1960–61	China
1962–63	China
1964–65	China
1966–67	Japan
1968–69	Japan
1970–71	China
1972–73	Sweden
1974–75	China

Gallery of Sportsmen

ALI, Mummahad. Ali changed his name from Cassius Clay when adopting the Muslim faith. Before that he was known as the 'Louisville Lip' because of his controversial utterances, in which he styled himself the 'Greatest'. Many good judges would agree with his assessment: he was certainly the greatest entertainer and most colourful character boxing has known.

He won an Olympic Gold Medal as an amateur before taking the world heavyweight title from Sonny Liston when only 22 years old. He was a good champion, beating all logical challengers, until his refusal to join the U.S. Army forced him out of the ring for three years. He announced his retirement, but came back by popular demand, only to suffer eventually his first defeat at the hands of the new champion Joe Frazier. He was past his best, but he regained the champion-ship from George Foreman in 1974 and continues to be boxing's biggest attraction.

BANKS, Gordon. After the victory of England in the World Cup of 1966, Gordon Banks was acclaimed by mutal consent as the 'best goalkeeper in the world'. It was not until the dying moments of the semi-final that he finally conceded a goal to Portugal, having kept his goal intact for nearly five matches. His reputation was enhanced in the World Cup finals of 1970, when one save he made from Pele became a classic in soccer legend. Unfortunately Banks was involved in a motor car accident in 1972 and badly injured his eyes, and although he has since played with the sight of only one imperfect eye, he was forced to retire from first-class soccer. However he remained in soccer as a coach.

BANNISTER, Roger. While a medical student at Oxford, Bannister ran his way into the history books when he won a mile race on the University's Iffley Road track in the time of 3 minutes, 59.4 seconds, on June 6, 1954. It was the first time that the magic four minutes had been beaten. Shrewd training had brought Bannister this success, and though John Landy broke the record shortly afterwards, Bannister showed that his run was no fluke by soundly beating Landy in the 1958 Empire Games mile.

BECKENBAUER, Franz. After the 1974 World Cup, Beckenbauer was at the top of the soccer world as captain of the champions, West Germany, and as captain of the German league champions and European Cup winners Bayern Munich. Born in 1945, Beckenbauer signed for Bayern at the age of thirteen. He has won league championship and cup winners medals, European Cup and European Cup Winners Cup medals, European Championship and World Cup medals. A centre defender or mid-field player, he is one of the world's best players.

BOYCOTT, Geoffrey. In the 1970 cricket season, Boycott became the first batsman to average over 100 runs for the English season. He scored 2,503 runs in 30 innings, 5 not out, to average 100.12. Born in 1940, he was awarded his Yorkshire cap in 1963 and first played for England in 1964. He scored 260 not out against Essex at Colchester in 1970, and his highest score in test cricket is 246 not out against India at Leeds in 1967. Boycott, an opening batsman, plays in contact lenses (for some years he played in spectacles) and is one of the most prolific run-scorers in the world.

BRADMAN, Sir Donald. Born in New South Wales in 1908, Bradman became almost a run-making machine in cricket. He only falls short of comparison with Sir Jack Hobbs in his inability to really master difficult wickets. Bradman scored a century in his first first-class appearance. He played in Australian cricket from 1927 to 1949. His career figures were 28,067 runs in 338 innings, averaging 95.14. He got 117 centuries, reached 200 37 times, and 300 six times. His top score of 452 not out stood as a world record for 29 years. He played in 52 test matches, 24 of them as captain. His test average was 99.94 including 29 centuries. Since his retirement, Sir Donald has worked as a journalist and test selector.

CHARLTON, Bobby. When he retired from soccer at the end of the 1972—73 season, Bobby Charlton had made over 600 league appearances for Manchester United, his only club, had played 106 times for England, a record later beaten by Bobby Moore, and had scored over 200 goals for his club and 49 for England, a record unlikely to be beaten for some years. A survivor of the Munich air crash, he won League Championship and F. A. cup medals and, his most prized

177

possession in view of the Munich disaster, a European Cup medal. He was European Footballer of the Year in 1966 and was awarded the O.B.E. in 1969. His exciting style, thunderous shooting and modest sporting demeanour made him Britain's best known and best loved footballer. He began playing again in 1974 as Preston's player-manager.

COMPTON, Denis. Compton was probably the most successful cricketer and footballer Britain has produced. As a right-hand bat and slow left-arm bowler, he played his first game for Middlesex in 1936, gaining his county cap the same year. Despite knee trouble towards the end of his career, Compton became a dashing bat and played in more than 70 Test matches. He scored 3,000 runs in one season and 2,000 on five occasions. His soccer career was with Arsenal, with whom he gained a League Championship medal (1947—48) and Cup Winner's medal (1949—50).

COOPER, Henry. Cooper was one of twin brothers who fought as amateurs and professionals, Henry eventually proving the better. He lost many early fights, and suffered greatly throughout his career with bad eye injuries. A knock-out of Dick Richardson when all seemed lost turned the tide, and Henry went on to win the British and Empire heavyweight titles in 1959. He held these titles for ten years, adding the European title to them, but his cut eye handicap lost him his world title fight with Cassius Clay. In an earlier fight he had almost knocked out Clay with his best punch, his famous left hook, affectionately known as 'Enery's 'ammer'. After a quarrel with the British Board of Control, he relinquished his titles and retired for a year, only to win them back again. He lost them for good in 1971 to Joe Bugner, a verdict with which most of the crowd disagreed. He was awarded the O.B.E., and his commonsense, sportsmanship and modesty, which came through during his many television appearances, made him the most popular of all British boxers.

CRUYFF, Johan. Before the 1974 World Cup, Cruyff was considered by most soccer experts to have succeeded Pele as the world's greatest player. In the event, he captained Holland into second place and confirmed his artistry. Born in 1946, he made his debut for Ajax of Amsterdam in the 1965—66 season and steered them to European Cup victories and to the World Club Championship. He made his debut for Holland in 1966. Cruyff's most exciting asset is his acceleration which takes him past even the quickest defenders. In the 1973—74 season he was transferred from Ajax to Barcelona for a world record transfer fee of about £ 1,000,000 and in his first season took Barcelona from near the bottom to the top of the Spanish league.

CURRY, John. At Innsbruck in 1976 John Curry became the first British male skater to win an Olympic gold medal. Curry also won the World and European championships, and not only proved himself the best in the world, but altered skating values, making artistic expression as necessary as athleticism and technical excellence. From Birmingham, Curry trained at Richmond before going to the United States, where sponsorship by a wealthy American, coaching by one of the world's top coaches and unlimited access to ice helped him to the top. He is now a professional and has founded a theatre of skating.

DI STEFANO, Alfredo. Real Madrid, the Spanish football team, reached a state of supremacy in European football during the early 1950s that is unlikely to be surpassed. They won the European Cup for the first five years it existed. No player helped the team more to reach this standard than Alfredo di Stefano (he scored in all five finals from the centre forward position, a superb goal-scorer with brilliant ball control). Born in the Argentine, Di Stefano had a short spell in Colombia before coming to Spain to play for Barcelona and finally settling with Real Madrid.

FANGIO, Juan Manuel. This Argentine racing driver was world champion in 1951, '54, '55, '56, and '57. For the whole decade he was the finest driver and, if he failed to win, it was more often the fault of the machine than the man. It is said that Stirling Moss styled himself on the relaxed Fangio.

179

As an example of his consistency, Fangio's record for the 1957 season was:—1st in the Monaco, Argentine, French and German Grands Prix, and 2nd in the Pescara and Italian Grands Prix.

FRY, C. B. Charles Burgess Fry was undoubtedly sport's finest all-rounder. Born in Croydon in 1872, he died in Hampstead in 1956, aged 84. Though principally known for his achievements at cricket, he played for England at soccer, for Southampton in the 1902 F.A. Cup Final, gained an athletic blue for Oxford and for 21 years held the world long jump record of 23'5". Fry only just failed to gain a rugby blue and there were other minor sports at which he excelled. His county cricket career spanned thirty years; he played in 26 test matches and on one occasion captained England. His academic career was just as brilliant as his remarkable sporting achievements.

GRACE, W. G. The first name one thinks of in cricket history, and well one might, for Grace's career figures of 54,896 runs, 2,876 wickets and 871 catches will probably never be equalled. Born in Bristol in 1848, Grace played for West Gloucestershire at the age of nine and made his first-class debut at seventeen. By the time he reached his last game in 1908, he had created more cricket records than any other player. He played in 22 tests, being captain 13 times. It is thought that in all the games he played in, he scored 80,000 runs and took 7,000 wickets. He died in 1915.

HARRIS, Reg. Harris was Britain's greatest world-class racing cyclist during the years following World War II. He became World Professional Sprint Champion in 1949, and held it for the two following years, then regained it in 1954. In 1951 he won the Trophie Gentil, the highest honour in international cycling, and despite the lack of interest in the sport in Britain (compared with the continental countries), he became Sportsman of the Year in 1949 and 1951. His Grand Prix victories include Copenhagen and Amsterdam (four times each) and Paris (twice). He came out of retirement in

1974 at the age of 53 and won the British Professional Sprint Championship.

HOBBS, Sir John ('Jack'). Recognised as possibly the finest batsman ever. Born at Cambridge in 1882, he played a few games for that county, then offered his services to Essex, who turned him down. Surrey accepted him, and from 1905 to 1934 he scored 61,237 runs (averaging 50.65) including 197 centuries. His test career lasted from 1907 to 1930, and included 5,410 runs at an average of 56.94. Besides topping the averages for many seasons, in 1920 he topped both the batting and bowling averages. This great Knight of Cricket died in 1963.

HUNT, James. In 1976 racing driver James Hunt won the World Championship, after the closest contest for years with Niki Lauda. Hunt, whose early days of racing earned him the nickname 'Hunt the Shunt' did his early Grand Prix racing with Hesketh Racing but switched to McLaren to win the title. When the Japanese Grand Prix, the last, began, Lauda was just ahead of Hunt, but Lauda's retirement meant that Hunt needed to finish fourth or better to win. He finished third, and followed fellow Britons Stewart, Clark, Hill, Surtees and Hawthorn as World Champion.

LAVER, Rod. When Laver won the Australian, French, United States and Wimbledon championships in 1969, he became the first player to win the "Grand Slam" twice. He had previously performed the feat in 1962 (Donald Budge is the only other player to achieve it). Laver was born in 1938 and reached the first of four consecutive Wimbledon finals aged twenty in 1959. He is not a big man but the power of his left-handed shots, particularly on the backhand, earned him the nickname of 'Rocket'. He turned professional after winning the Wimbledon championship in 1961 and 1962, but returned to take two more Wimbledon titles in 1968 and 1969 when the championships became open to professionals. He was awarded the MBE in 1970.

LOUIS, Joe. (Real name Joseph Barrow.) He was born in

Alabama in 1914, became a professional boxer at 20 and won his first 27 fights. In 1936, Louis had become a sure prospect for the World Heavyweight Championship, but unaccountably lost to Max Schmeling. Two years later he won the title by defeating James Braddock. In the return with Schmeling, champion Louis took only 2 minutes 4 seconds to beat him. Louis remained undefeated champion until 1949, when he retired after 25 successful defences of his title. Only three challengers had stayed the distance against the mighty Louis. A come-back to the ring, to help pay tax debts, failed.

MATTHEWS, Sir Stan. Possibly the greatest name in soccer, Stan Matthews was born at Hanley, in the Potteries. He joined Stoke City as a professional at the age of 17, after being a prodigy in schoolboy international football. His famous body-swerve and ball control turned him into a living legend and he proved the biggest box office draw ever. At the age of 47 he was transferred to Blackpool, but returned to his original club of Stoke City in 1961—62. Matthews first played for England during the 1934—35 season at the age of 19. His last international appearance was in 1956—57. In all he made 84 international appearances. In 1957, he was voted Footballer of the Year, and in 1958 he got the C.B.E. for his services to sport. Returned to help his old club, Stoke City, in 1961, and was knighted in 1965.

MOORE, Bobby. The third Englishman to play over 100 times for his country, Bobby Moore in 1973 broke all soccer records by hoisting his total of internationals to 107. An outstanding player since his teens, Moore also played eighteen times for the England Youth team and eight times for the Under-23 team. He made his debut for West Ham United in 1958, when 17, and played for England in the 1962 World Cup finals. He first captained his country in 1963, and led England to the World Cup victory of 1966, when he was elected player of the tournament. He captained England again in the 1970 World Cup finals. A superb defender, he is extremely strong, rarely loses a tackle, and his calm unruffled play is an inspiration to his side. He was transferred to Fulham in 1974.

NICKLAUS, Jack. On records alone Jack Nicklaus is the greatest golfer the world has known. When he won the U.S.P.G.A. tournament in 1973 he beat Boby Jones' record of 13 major tournament wins which had stood since 1930. He has yet to achieve the ultimate in golf—the winning of the British and American Opens, the U.S. Masters and the U.S. P.G.A. tournaments in the same year—it is a measure of his greatness that each year it seems possible that he will do it, and the feeling exists that if Nicklaus cannot do it, nobody can. A strong, powerful athlete, he can hit the ball as far as anybody, yet he retains a delicate touch around the greens. He avoids being thought of as an automaton by his grace and sportsmanship, and he is immensely popular, all over the world.

OWENS, Jesse. This coloured American became the greatest sprinter of them all and dominated an Olympic Games more than any man has done since. An athlete of superb build and economy of movement, he had no equal over the short distances. By the time of the 1936 Olympic Games in Berlin, Owens held the world records for the 100 yards, 100 metres, 200 metres, 220 yards, 200 metres hurdles, 220 yards hurdles and the long jump. Hitler came to the Games to see German dominance. Instead, he saw the greatest one-man show of all time when Jesse Owens won the 100 metres, 200 metres, long jump and gained a fourth gold medal with the winning U.S. team in the 4×100 metres relay.

PALMER, Arnold. Arnold Palmer emerged as a great golfer in the early 1960s when golf was booming all over the world. His great talent and his bold manner of playing the game quickly made him one of the world's best known, most popular and rich sportsmen. A great competitor, and a great winner, he has won all the major tournaments, and over a million dollars in prize money. His regular gallery, who follow him hole by hole through tournament after tournament, became known as 'Arnie's Army' and he brought the concept of the 'charge' to golf: a patch of brilliant play which would carry him to the top of the scoreboard. With Nicklaus and Player he formed what was called the 'Big Three' of golf.

PELE. Born Edson Arantes Do Nascimento in 1941, this great footballer, acknowledged by many to be the greatest-ever, is known throughout the world simply as 'Pele'. An international at 16, Pele first attracted the notice of the world when as a seventeen-year-old he scored two goals in the World Cup Final, one of them still talked of with awe—he flicked the ball over a defender's head, caught it on his thigh, repeated the performance and volleyed the ball home. In 1970, when Brazil won the World Cup again, he astonished the world with another piece of sheer virtuosity, almost scoring against Czechoslovakia from his own half. Pele scored his 1000th goal, a record, in 1969. A complete footballer, with more than a touch of genius, he announced his retirement from International football in 1970, but his name will live for as long as soccer lasts.

PIGGOTT, Lester. Britain's greatest jockey since Gordon Richards, Lester Piggott is essentially a man for the big occasion, as his record of riding 20 Classic winners, including six Derby winners, testifies. Piggott comes from a racing family, his father Keith having been a trainer and jockey, as were both his grandfathers, and he has uncles who won the Derby. Lester was riding at three years old, rode his first winner at 12 and his first Derby winner at 18. Piggott's main assets as a jockey are his strength and boldness, his dashing style often getting him into trouble in his younger days. The fight to keep his weight down has persuaded Piggott to cut down the number of his rides in recent years, but he has been nine times champion jockey, and is acknowledged as the best throughout racing.

PLAYER, Gary. A South African born in 1935 Player became with Palmer and Nicklaus one of the so-called "Big Three"

184

of world golf. Dedication and a strong belief in physical fitness bring Player his successes which include the British Open Championship in 1959, '68 and '74, the U.S. Open Championship in 1965, the U.S. Masters in 1971 and '74, and the U.S. P.G.A. in 1962. He is the only South African to have won all four major championships.

PUSKAS, Feranc. Hungary's captain when they came to England in 1953, he led his national team to a 6—3 win. It was the first time a foreign team had beaten England in England. Puskas was a Hungarian Army officer who played as inside forward for his country. All the team relied on brilliant ball control to win. Puskas had this plus a left-foot shot that was one of the best in the world. Under his leadership, Hungary became the finest team in the world and might well have won the 1954 World Cup had it not been for an injury to Puskas in the Final when they were two goals up to Germany. When the Hungarian Revolution broke out in 1956, Puskas left his country and joined the famed Real Madrid. Alongside of Di Stefano, Puskas produced his previous best, despite his age.

RICHARDS, Sir Gordon. His record speaks for itself: Champion jockey 26 times, the first in 1925 and the last in 1953; and 4,870 winners. No jockey has matched that record and there was probably none so popular as the diminutive Sir Gordon. All his life the Derby had eluded him. Many thought that a Derby win was beyond him until 1953, when he eventually won on Pinza, to the delight of the whole racing world. When Sir Gordon finished riding, he became a successful trainer.

ROBINSON, Sugar Ray. Many boxing writers regard Sugar Ray Robinson (born Walker Smith) as the greatest pound-for-pound fighter of all time. A supreme artist, his career lasted 25 years and spanned 202 fights, and when he retired in 1965 at 45 years of age, he bore no marks, physical or mental, from his quarter of a century of fighting the world's best. He won the world welterweight title, and then with increasing weight won and lost the world middleweight championship five times—a record. He attempted to emulate Bob Fitzsimmons and Henry Armstrong by winning a world title at three weights when he challenged light heavyweight champion Joey Maxim, but after looking a winner for twelve rounds he collapsed in his corner, exhausted by the temperature of 104°. He is the best example of a complete boxer.

SOBERS, Gary. Garfield St. Aubrun Sobers is the greatest all-round cricketer the world has seen. At his peak the best batsman in the world, he was also in the top flight as a bowler. An exciting left-handed batsman he hits the ball hard all round the wicket. He bowls well in two styles, either swinging the new ball or bowling slower spinners. He captained West Indies. Two records he holds are the highest score in Test cricket—365 not out against Pakistan in 1958, and the highest score from a six-ball over—all six balls bowled to him by Nash of Glamorgan were hit for six in a county match in 1968. In 1974 he announced his retirement from full-time cricket.

VIREN, Lasse. Viren is a forestry policeman in Finland and a hero in a land famous for its great athletes since Paavo Nurmi. In the 1972 Olympic Games in Munich Viren won both the 5,000 metres and 10,000 metres, actually winning the latter after he'd been knocked over in the final. He achieved little between 1972 and 1976, but then appeared at the Montreal Olympics to repeat his wins in both events, running fifth in the marathon for good measure. Viren is young enough to win again at the 1980 games, but has already established himself as one of the greatest modern athletes.

WILDE, Jimmy. Weighing little over 7 stone, this Pontypridd flyweight started boxing in the old classic tradition. Over 700 boxing booth fights produced a superb fighting machine and a boxer with the hardest punch that had ever been seen at his weight. Wilde won the British title in 1916 by beating Joe Symonds. In the same year, the Americans sent over their world champion, Young Zulu Kid. Wilde K.O.'d him in 11 rounds to take the World Flyweight Championship—a title he held until 1923.

186

ZÁTOPEK, Emil. This Czech Army Officer won the 10,000 metres in the 1948 Olympic Games in London. It was not until he started producing world record times with apparent ease after this performance that the athletic world focused its attention on his training methods. They found that Zátopek was covering phenomenal distances each week in his torturous training schedules. It led to many of his contemporaries adopting this technique with success. Zátopek was the dominating runner in the 1952 Olympics, winning the 5,000 and 10,000 metres, and finally running away with the Marathon race.

PEOPLE AND LEISURE

Here are some of the dozens of spare-time activities which may appeal to you—ranging from camping to stamp collecting, from model-making to keeping tortoises.

Use of the Road

The open road is yours—on your bicycle or on foot—but your right to use it involves responsibilities on your part in return.

Cyclists, though they don't have to pass a driving test, must be fully aware of the Highway Code for their own safety as well as that of others. They are also obliged *by law* to have efficient brakes on *both* wheels, and a means of warning (either a bell or a horn). After dark they *must* have a head-lamp, a red tail-lamp and a red reflector at the rear. Cyclists are also advised to wear light-coloured clothes at night—and this is a safety measure for those on foot as well, particularly in country districts where because of the absence of a pavement it is necessary to walk along the edge of the road. Whenever walking on the road, whether by day or by night, you should *face* the oncoming traffic.

Cyclists should give clear hand-signals before making left or right turns, by raising the appropriate arm shoulder-high. On slowing down or stopping, the correct signal is an up-and-down movement of the right arm.

What the Highway Code tells you can be roughly summarised as follows:

For Pedestrians

1. Where there is no footpath, walk *facing* oncoming traffic.
2. Before crossing the road, look right, look left, then look

188

right again. Cross at right-angles, use zebra crossings, central refuges or other pedestrian aids whenever possible, and take extra care if your view is limited or blocked in any way.
3. Before stepping onto a zebra crossing, allow approaching traffic ample time to stop. Remember that when a zebra crossing has a central refuge each half of the crossing must be treated separately.
4. At junctions, always watch for vehicles turning the corner.
5. If there is a police officer controlling traffic, be guided by his signals.
6. Do not get on or off any moving vehicle.

For Cyclists

1. When moving off, make the signal for a right turn before pulling out from the kerb.
2. Keep well to the left, except when overtaking or turning right.
3. Always, in riding at night, make sure you could pull up within the range of your lights. If dazzled by oncoming lights, slow down or stop.
4. Slow down before bends and sharp corners.
5. Give way to pedestrians on zebra crossings. They have the legal right of way. At crossings controlled by lights or police, give way to pedestrians already on the crossing when the signal to move is given.
6. When making a turn at a junction, remember that pedestrians who are crossing have the right of way.
7. Look out for pedestrians on country roads, and give them ample room, particularly at left-hand bends.
8. Go slow when passing animals, and give them plenty of room.
9. Do not overtake near corners, road junctions or pedestrian crossings, or when approaching the brow of a hill, a humpback bridge or a narrower section of road. Be extremely careful about overtaking at dusk or in fog.

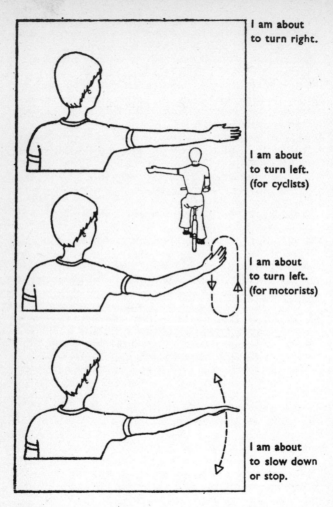

I am about
to turn right.

I am about
to turn left.
(for cyclists)

I am about
to turn left.
(for motorists)

I am about
to slow down
or stop.

10. Overtake on the right, except when the driver or rider in front has signalled that he intends to turn right.
11. Never cross a continuous white line along the middle of the road unless you can see a clear road ahead.
12. When approaching a road junction where there is a 'Slow' sign, slow down and be prepared to stop if necessary. At a 'Halt' sign you *must* stop at the major road, even if it is clear.
13. To turn right, signal in good time and take up a position just left of the middle of the road. For left turns keep over to the left, signal well in advance and avoid swinging out to the right.
14. When you draw up, pull in close to the near side of the road.
15. When riding, glance behind before you signal, move off, change course, overtake or turn.
16. Slow down, look both ways and listen carefully before going through a railway level crossing that has no gates. When there are unattended gates, open both gates before crossing, then close them after you. *Do not stop on the lines.* Never cross the lines when a warning signal is flashing or when the barriers have not lifted after the passing of a train—another train may be on the way.
17. If there is a track for cycles, use it.
18. *Never* ride more than two abreast, carry anything which could interfere with your control of your bicycle, hold on to another vehicle or cyclist, or ride close behind a moving vehicle.
19. It is against the law to stop a bicycle within the limits of a pedestrian crossing, except in circumstances beyond your control or to avoid an accident.
20. It is illegal to ride on a footpath, or to carry a passenger on a bicycle not built or adapted for more than one.
21. It is illegal to ride recklessly, to interrupt the free passage of another road user or to leave your cycle on the road in such a way that it could cause danger to others.

Here are some of the road signs with their meanings:

WARNING SIGNS

| ⊤ junction | Series of bends | Distance to STOP sign ahead | Distance to GIVE WAY sign ahead | Slippery road | Low-flying aircraft or sudden aircraft noise |

REGULATORY SIGNS

| | Ahead only | No entry | Maximum speed limit 70 mph | Maximum speed limit | Total weight limit |

INFORMATORY SIGNS

'Count-down' markers at exit from motorway or primary route (each bar represents 100 yards to the exit)

Advance warning of no through road

Appropriate traffic lanes at junction ahead

Country Code

1. Avoid dangers of fire. Be sure any cooking fires are extinguished before you move on.
2. Fasten all gates after use.
3. Keep dogs under control.
4. When crossing farm land keep to the path.
5. Do not damage fences, hedges or walls.
6. Leave no litter. You can be heavily fined for leaving rubbish behind.
7. Protect wild life, plants and trees.
9. Respect the countryside.

192

Angling

Angling might conveniently be divided into three categories: coarse, game and sea. Coarse fishing is fishing for all those species which live in fresh water, i.e. rivers, streams, lakes, reservoirs, gravel pits. Game fishing is concerned with those fish which are caught for eating, such as salmon and trout, which are also caught in fresh water. Sea fishing, of course, is fishing from piers, beaches or boats for those fish which live in the sea.

There are many methods of angling with rod and line. They can be divided into float-fishing and fly-fishing. In float-fishing the bait is suspended in the water or trailed along the bed, the movement of the float indicating a bite. Fly-fishing is the casting of an artificial fly on to the surface of the water.

Bait can be anything the fish is likely to eat. Maggots, worms, bread: almost anything can be used, and one of the pleasures of angling is the experimenting with baits. Artificial baits are also used, such as painted models of minnows or small fish.

Fly-fishing is a very skilful art. Accurate casting calls for much practice. Making the flies, called fly-tying, is also something which calls for practice and delicate skill.

An aspiring angler should study the water in which he intends to fish to discover which species are to be found there, and then he should study the habits of the fish themselves, to discover where in the water they are likely to be found, which bait is likely to be successful, and the best methods of fishing for them. Ground-baiting is a useful preliminary tactic. The bait to be used should be freely placed in the stretch of water to be fished, called the "swim", to accustom the fish to taking it before the hooked bait is cast into the water. The size of hook and strength of line should also be considered with regard to the species to be caught.

Some of the most notable British fish to be caught are

given in the attached list. Many are not officially recognized as record fish because the conditions relating to record catches were not observed.

Species	Weight	Location	Year
Barbel	16lb 1oz (7,320 gr.)	Hampshire Avon	1960
Bleak	5¼oz (150 gr.)	Radcliffe on Trent	1890
Bream (common)	13lb 8oz (6,140 gr.)	Chiddingstone Castle Lake	1945
Bream (silver)	4lb 8oz (2,040 gr.)	Tortworth Lake	1923
Carp	44lb (20,980 gr.)	Redmire Pool	1952
Carp (Crucian)	4lb 15½oz (2,250 gr.)	Johnson's Lake	1972
Chub	10lb 8oz (4,760 gr.)	River Annan	1955
Dace	1lb 8¾oz (700 gr.)	River Derwent	1947
Eel	8lb 10oz (3,910 gr.)	Hunstrete Lake	1969
Grayling	4lb 8oz (2,040 gr.)	River Wylye	1955
Gudgeon	4¼oz (120 gr.)	River Thames	1933
Perch	5lb 15oz (2,690 gr.)	Suffolk Stour	1949
Pike	53lb (24,040 gr.)	Lough Conn	1920
Roach	3lb 14oz (1,760 gr.)	Lambeth Reservoir	1938
Rudd	4lb 8oz (2,040 gr.)	Thetford	1933
Salmon	69lb 12oz (31,640 gr.)	River Tweed	1730
Tench	9lb 1oz (4,110 gr.)	Hemingford Grey (gravel pit)	1963
Trout (brown)	39lb 8oz (17,920 gr.)	Loch Awe	1866
Trout (rainbow)	10lb 0½oz (4,540 gr.)	Kings Lynn (lake)	1970
Zander	15lb 5oz (6,940 gr.)	Great Ouse Relief Channel	1971

Camping

Camping can be one of the most pleasant and rewarding of summer recreations, but a camping trip may be spoilt if some necessary item has been omitted from the gear, or, on the other hand, if you overload yourself by carrying things you don't need. The following checklist should prove helpful when you plan your camping trip.

Personal Equipment

Rucksack	Flannel
Change of clothing	Soap
Change of underclothing	Toothbrush and paste
2 spare pairs of socks	Brush and comb
Spare pair of shoes	Nail brush
Spare shoelaces	Maps
Pair of pyjamas	Metal mirror
Handkerchiefs	Compass
Mackintosh	Pocket-knife
Warm pullover	Water-bottle
Swimming costume	Money
Towel (possibly 2)	

Equipment Shared among the Party

Tent
Tent-pegs
Cord
Small spade or trowel
Axe
Groundsheets
Sleeping bags (or blankets)
Spare blankets (if desired)
Inflatable mattresses and pillows
Torch, with spare batteries
Cooking stove
Fuel and matches
Stewing-pot, frying-pan and kettle
Plastic, aluminium or paper plates and mugs

Cutlery
Teacloth
Can and bottle opener
Food box (for perishable items)
Canvas bucket for washing
Small First Aid kit

Tents

If you are buying a tent for your trip, you will find illustrated below some of the many varieties from which to make a choice.

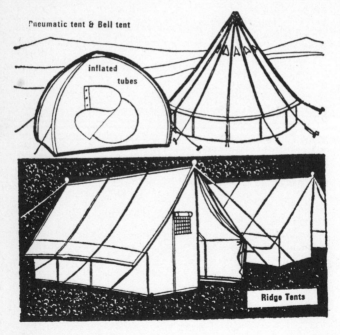

Pneumatic tent & Bell tent

inflated tubes

Ridge Tents

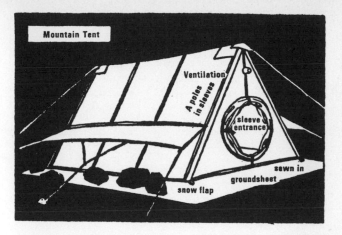

Mountain Tent

Ventilation

A poles in sleeve

sleeve entrance

sewn in groundsheet

snow flap

Youth Hostels

Hikers and cyclists wanting to use Youth Hostels can get full details of membership from their National Headquarters.

The rules vary slightly from country to country. In Britain you can join the Youth Hostels Association from the age of five onwards. Up to the age of nine you must be accompanied by a parent or legal guardian when using Youth Hostels, and up to twelve by any adult member. From twelve onwards members may use the Hostels without being accompanied.

There is a family membership scheme whereby children from five to sixteen are enrolled free if both parents join. If you live in England or Wales, your membership will be valid all over the world. There are nearly 3,000 Hostels on the Continent alone. You may stay up to three consecutive nights at any one Hostel. Most Hostels provide meals at low charges; alternatively, cooking facilities are available. A list of National H.Q. addresses follows:—

England and Wales: Y.H.A., National Office, Trevelyan House, St. Albans, Herts.

Scotland: S.Y.H.A., 7 Glebe Crescent, Stirling.

Northern Ireland: Y.H.A.N.I., 93 Dublin Road, Belfast.

Republic of Ireland: An Oige, 39 Mountjoy Square, Dublin.

Australia: 184, Sussex Street, Sydney, New South Wales, 2000.

New Zealand: N.Z.Y.H.A., P.O. Box 436, Christchurch. C 1.

South Africa: P.O. Box 4402, Capetown, South Africa.

Canada: 333, River Road, Vanier City, Ottawa, K1L 8BN, Ontario.

United States: American Youth Hostel Incorporated, National Campus, Delaplane, Virginia, 22025.

FIRST AID WHEN OUT AND ABOUT

When giving First Aid remember that unless you've had training through the Red Cross or some similar organisation you may do more harm by doing too much than too little. Your attempts to treat serious burns or to straighten a fracture may make it more difficult for the doctor who later has to cure the patient.

The *first* object of First Aid is to save life: that is, to prevent the casualty from dying before medical aid can be obtained. Therefore, look immediately for signs of asphyxia or severe bleeding and, if necessary, stop bleeding and begin artificial respiration. *Every second counts.*

The *second* object is to prevent any deterioration in the condition of the casualty. This is achieved by attending to the injuries which the casualty has sustained, and preventing further injury.

Never attempt to give an unconscious person anything to drink.

ASPHYXIA

Asphyxia is a condition whereby air is prevented from entering the lungs of the body such as by Suffocation, Drowning, Gas, Choking and Strangulation.

Asphyxia can also occur in cases of electric shock.

If the casualty has stopped breathing do not lose an instant, act quickly and methodically.

1. Clear away any obstruction round the neck or face, or within the mouth or throat.
2. Lay the casualty on his back and kneel beside his head.
3. Place one hand under his neck and the other hand on top of his head.
4. Lift the neck and tilt the head backwards as far as possible; this may clear the airway and the casualty may begin to breathe. If he does not, immediately commence artifical respiration.

ARTIFICIAL RESPIRATION

Mouth to Mouth Method

1. Keep the head tilted well backwards.
2. With one hand pinch the patient's nose shut and keep his head bent back. With the other hold his chin to keep his mouth open (but do not let fingers get in the way of the mouth or press on the neck).
3. Open your mouth wide, seal the casualty's mouth with your own and blow in smoothly.
4. Watch out of the corner of your eye, if possible, for the rise of the chest. Now remove your mouth to allow the air out again and the chest to fall. At the same time you take another breath in.
5. Repeat 3 and 4 as soon as his chest has fallen; for a baby or small child blow gently and carefully. In no circumstances blow violently into a baby's lungs.

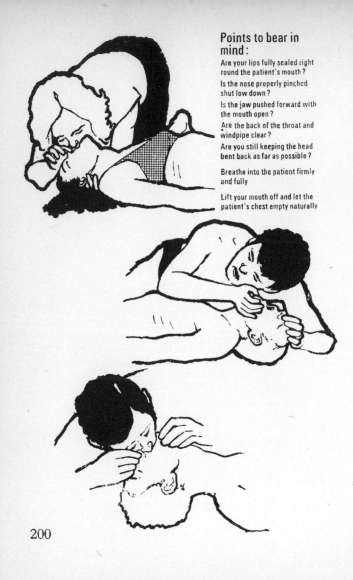

Points to bear in mind:

Are your lips fully sealed right round the patient's mouth?

Is the nose properly pinched shut low down?

Is the jaw pushed forward with the mouth open?

Are the back of the throat and windpipe clear?

Are you still keeping the head bent back as far as possible?

Breathe into the patient firmly and fully

Lift your mouth off and let the patient's chest empty naturally

Revised Holger Nielsen Method

1. Lay casualty face down with head turned to one side, arms above his head with elbows bent so that the upper part of the cheek is resting on his hands and his mouth clear of the ground.
2. Kneel at his head, placing one knee near casualty's head and one foot alongside his elbow.
3. Place your hands over casualty's shoulder blades, with thumbs touching in the mid-line and fingers spread out, the arms being kept straight.
4. Rock forward gently with arms straight and let pressure be applied by weight of upper part of body only (see Fig. 1).
5. Rock back with arms straight, as you slide your hands to just below the elbows of casualty (see Fig. 2).
6. Continue to rock back so lifting casualty's arms until tension is felt (see Fig. 3), to cause inhalation.
7. Then lower casualty's arms down and place your hands on his back as in Fig. 1.
8. Repeat the above movement with rhythmic rocking at the rate of 12 times a minute, until breathing has been re-established.
9. If the arms are injured, place them by the sides of the body then do the complete procedure, but insert your hands under the casualty's shoulders and raise them for inhalation.

DROWNING

Do not lose an instant; act quickly and methodically.
1. Quickly clear mouth of any false teeth, weeds, or obvious obstruction.
2. Give mouth to mouth artificial respiration as described opposite and on previous page.

201

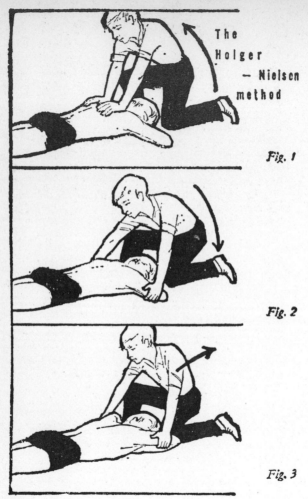

The
Holger
— Nielsen
method

Fig. 1

Fig. 2

Fig. 3

3. Maintain body heat of patient by placing rug or coat over and under him and continue artificial respiration until a doctor has pronounced the patient dead.
4. When consciousness returns, keep casualty lying down in recovery position and treat for shock (on next page).

ELECTRIC SHOCK

Act promptly, taking care not to electrocute yourself.
1. Switch off current if possible or unplug cable.
2. If this is not possible stand on an insulating material (a dry rubber mackintosh, or piece of wood) and pull casualty away by means of rope or walking stick, but not an umbrella which has metal ribs. If possible avoid contact with the casualty's armpits.
3. Apply Mouth to Mouth Resuscitation if breathing has stopped. Beware of fractures and burnt areas.
Note: Very high-powered currents (pylon wires, power stations) can be very dangerous if approached: keep clear and do not attempt rescue until current is known to have been cut off.

BLEEDING OR HAEMORRHAGE

Mild bleeding

Act immediately.
Treat it as a wound (page 208): firm bandage pressure will cope with it.

Severe bleeding (fast and dangerous)

With fingers and thumb press the wound edges firmly together. Keep this pressure at least ten minutes to let a clot form. Raise a bleeding arm or leg (but not if it could be fractured). Replace your finger pressure by that of a firm dressing pad and bandage as soon as you can. Keep the

How to protect oneself from lightning
If there is no shelter available, keep away from

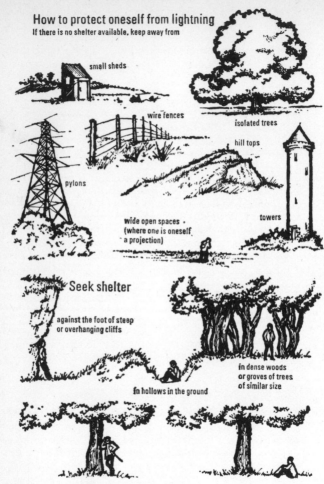

small sheds

isolated trees

wire fences

hill tops

pylons

wide open spaces
(where one is oneself
a projection)

towers

Seek shelter

against the foot of steep
or overhanging cliffs

in dense woods
or groves of trees
of similar size

in hollows in the ground

If you have only one tree in an open space
DO NOT lean against it but keep several feet away and do not touch it

injured part at rest. If blood continues to ooze through the bandage leave the bandage on and add more padding and firm bandaging over it.

SHOCK PREVENTION

In any serious injury:
1. Stop any bleeding.
2. Lay casualty on his back with head to one side and legs slightly raised, unless they are fractured.
3. Loosen clothing at neck and waist.
4. Maintain body heat of casualty by placing rug or coat around casualty. Do not give anything to drink or apply hot water bottles.
5. Handle as gently as possible and avoid any unnecessary movements.
6. See there is plenty of fresh air, and protect against any inclemency of weather.
7. Be cheerful and encouraging.
8. Get a doctor as soon as possible.

FAINTING

1. If the casualty feels faint, sit him down and lower his head between the knees.
2. Loosen clothing at neck and waist.
3. Allow plenty of fresh air, but protect from cold.
4. When casualty regains strength gradually raise him and give sips of water, tea or coffee.
5. If he becomes unconscious, act as below.

UNCONSCIOUSNESS: THE RECOVERY POSITION

1. Examine the casualty to see that:
   (a) He is breathing — If not apply artificial respiration (see page 199).

205

(b) He is not bleeding — If he is give appropriate treatment.
2. If you suspect fractures which would prevent moving him, turn the head to one side and ensure a clear airway by tilting the head slightly backwards.
3. If he can be moved, put him into the Recovery Position; turn patient on to side; the lower leg and arm are stretched out behind him. The upper arm and leg should be bent so that the hip and elbow joints are at about a right angle. The head should be tilted slightly backwards
4. Do not give patient anything to drink.

BURNS AND SCALDS

Never handle a burned area and do not apply any lotions or ointment. The object of treatment of burns is to reduce the heat of the burn.
1. Place the burned area in cool clean water for at least ten minutes and until pain is relieved.
2. Apply a clean dry dressing.
3. Arrange for transport to hospital as soon as possible. The transport of a seriously burned patient to hospital should not be delayed.
4. Burn blisters should not be pricked.
5. Reassure the casualty, as this is most important to his recovery. Guard against shock (page 205).

FRACTURES

Do not move casualty until injured part is immobilised, unless life is in immediate danger from surrounding environment, i.e. falling buildings, fire etc.

Closed (Bone not exposed)

1. Ensure casualty is in comfortable condition.
2. Keep warm, handle gently and generally guard against shock (see page 205).

The Recovery Position
Lying on one side.
Head bent back; face bent down.
Upper arm bent at right angle to shoulder
and elbow; upper hand near the face.
Upper leg bent at right angle at hip and knee.
Lower arm and leg stretched out behind.

3. Immobilise injured part by means of bandages and slings. The chest wall or the sound leg serve as good splints. In certain circumstances well padded splints may be required.
    (a) In the case of an arm, apply padding; bandage and support arm in a sling with the elbow bent and hand pointing to uninjured shoulder. If elbow itself is fractured, keep arm straight.
    (b) If a leg, pad well between the knees and ankles; bandage the sound leg to the injured one.
4. Never try to set the bones.
5. Do not give food or drink, as anaesthetic may have to be given shortly.

Get a doctor or send to hospital quickly.

Open (Wound exposes Bone)

Treat as for a simple fracture but, in addition:
1. Cover the wound with a dry dressing.
2. Stop any bleeding (see pages 203).
3. Especially take care to counteract shock.

Note : Do not try to push protruding bone back into place.

DISLOCATIONS

1. Support the limb in the most comfortable position. Use plenty of padding with bandages. Never attempt to reduce a dislocation.
2. Reassure the casualty which will help to control shock.
3. Guard against shock (see page 205).
4. In cases of the lower jaw, remove any dentures if possible and support the jaw by a bandage tied over the top of the head.
5. Transfer patient to hospital.

SPRAINS AND STRAINS

1. Immobilise injured part.
2. Apply cold compress where possible.
3. Do not remove shoe or boot, unless swelling of the foot is great.
4. Arrange for transport to hospital.
5. If there is any doubt as to the extent of the injury treat as a fracture.

POISONING

Poisons fall into two categories.
(a) Those poisons which burn.
(b) Those which do not burn.

Unconscious Casualty

1. Ensure he is breathing freely; place him in the Recovery Position.
2. Should he not be breathing commence artificial respiration at once.
3. Tranfer to hospital immediately.

Conscious Casualty

1. Ask the casualty exactly what happened.
2. (a) If there are no stains on the lips or mouth (indicating burning), make him vomit, by giving him to drink 2 tablespoons of salt to a glass of water. Repeat this once.
   (b) If there are stains, DO NOT make him vomit, but dilute the poison by giving slow drinks of water, milk or barley water.
3. Transfer casualty to hospital at once without delay.
Note : In all cases of poisoning any bottles or other containers found must be sent with the casualty to hospital.

SNAKE BITES

Generally speaking the only poisonous snake to be found in the wild state in Great Britain is the Adder, which is characteristically recognised by zig-zag lines on the snake's back.

1. It is very important to reassure the patient.
2. Lay the casualty down at absolute rest.
3. Put a clean dry dressing over the point.
4. Splint the affected limb as for a fracture.
5. Transport the casualty to hospital as a stretcher case.

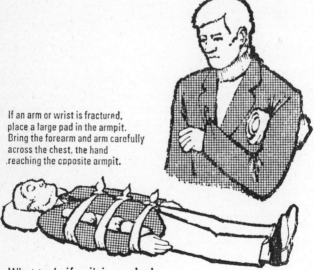

If an arm or wrist is fractured, place a large pad in the armpit. Bring the forearm and arm carefully across the chest, the hand reaching the opposite armpit.

What to do if a rib is cracked

Padding between the limb and the body. Broad bandages should be placed round the upper arm and the body, just below the elbow and the body, and round the wrist and thigh.

Sketching and Painting

This is a hobby that can give anyone a great deal of enjoyment and satisfaction—even if he has always felt that he 'can't draw a straight line'. In fact, it is often those having the greatest doubts as to their ability who eventually produce the best results. Painting and drawing are wonderful ways of increasing your powers of observation, and they can provide a far more personal record of the things you see than the camera can ever hope to achieve.

For pencil sketching a beginner needs a range of soft and hard pencils, some sticks of soft charcoal, a block or book of cartridge paper, a soft india-rubber and a charcoal eraser. A small bottle of charcoal fixative, together with a blower, will be needed to 'fix' charcoal drawings.

Art classes at school may have taught the chief rule of perspective; briefly, it is that distant objects appear smaller. If you stand in the middle of a railway track and look along it, the two rails appear to draw closer together in the distance. This applies to all objects; the wall of a house, viewed at an angle, appears taller at the end nearest the point at which you are standing. Easy practice in perspective can be had by sketching open country with fields. Trees, hedges and fences will give you a challenge in perspective which will stand you in good stead when you tackle something more difficult.

Light and shade in pencil sketching are achieved by depth of pencil shading. There is no need to pay too much attention to the way in which this shading is applied, or to try to put in a great many details. The best way to begin is to look for the main masses of light and dark in front of you and to try to represent their shapes, as well as their sizes and tones in relation to one another. The more outstanding details that you see can be put in later. You should, however, bear in mind that a sketch of a scene is always a simplification of that scene.

Drawing in perspective

level view

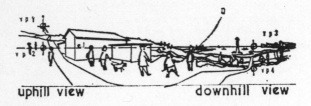

uphill view   **downhill view**

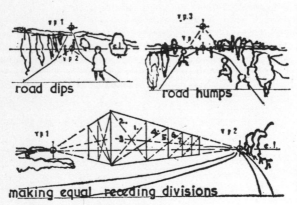

road dips   **road humps**

making equal receding divisions

V.P. = vanishing point
e.l. = eye level - of viewer
1,2,3,4,5,6,7. = order of construction lines

212

Should you wish to sketch in pen and ink—a more limiting medium for a beginner—you will need a harder-sufaced paper, a small range of nibs and a bottle of black India ink. You can also buy India ink in a variety of colours.

If you would like to try painting, you may choose to start with oil paints, water-colours, poster colours or even pastels. If you are beginning in oils, you will find prepared hardboard a satisfactory surface to use and inexpensive compared with canvas. It is best to equip yourself with large brushes, to use a good-sized surface, and to treat the subject matter broadly, looking for areas of colours and tones, and for their relations to one another. Try some exercises which will help you to see how one colour affects another; place patches of different colours, or of different shades of one colour, next to each other and study the effect. Some colours are heavier than others; some come forward while others seem to recede; some combinations of colours are harmonious while some are discordant. All of these discoveries can be applied to your painting. Many other colour exercises can be found in the various books on painting which are in your public library.

You may find it useful to keep to a fairly small selection of colours at first. The following is a suggested basic palette for oil painting:

Cadmium Yellow
Cadmium Red
Alizarin Crimson
Monastral Blue
Ultramarine (blue)
Viridian (green)
Flake, Titanium or Zinc White
Ivory Black

Useful colours to add to this are Yellow Ochre, Light Red, Cobalt Blue and Terre Verte (earth green).

Film Sizes

Standard film sizes in general use for ordinary photography are the following:

Film Size (millimetres)	Pictures per Film	Size of Picture (inches)
35	36	$1 \times 1\frac{1}{2}$
127	16	$1\frac{1}{8} \times 1\frac{3}{4}$
127	12	$1\frac{3}{4} \times 1\frac{3}{4}$
127	8	$2\frac{1}{4} \times 1\frac{3}{4}$
120 and 620	16	$2\frac{1}{4} \times 1\frac{5}{9}$
120 and 620	12	$2\frac{1}{4} \times 2\frac{1}{4}$
120 and 620	8	$2\frac{1}{4} \times 3\frac{1}{4}$

Standard sizes of cine-film in general use are: 8, 9.5, 16 and 35 millimetres.

Film Scripting

The economical sizes of cine-film for amateurs are 8 and 9.5 millimetres. Silent film in both cases is exposed at 16 'frames' or pictures per second and projected at the same speed. Spoken commentaries for silent film should be based on a calculation of 3 words per second. Preparation of a running commentary is done by means of a table made on the following lines:

Scene	Seconds	Aggregate Seconds	Commentary
G/V * Fishing village	3	3	Throughout Cornwall we found small fishing villages, most with only three
M/S Moored boats	2	5	or four boats.
C/U Elderly fisherman	3	8	Each boat is a family concern. This seventy-

M/CU Dad talks to him	2	10	year-old skipper told my father that he'd been at sea since he was only
C/U Hands Dad fish	6	16	eight—and gave Dad an odd-looking fish like an octopus!
T/S Deck of boat	2	18	They were unloading; most of the fish is sent up
L/V Wagons at dockside	4	22	to London by rail straight away.
C/U Curious fish	3	25	But we didn't send *our* odd fish! When
M/S Fish into hole; Mother holding her			the skipper wasn't looking we
nose		29	dug a hole and buried it!

This family adventure, running half a minute approximately, takes just over a third of a 'roll' of 9.5 millimetre film, and a much smaller proportion in the case of 8 millimetre film.

*Key to Standard Abbreviations used in Film Scripting

G/V = General view
L/V = Long view
M/S = Medium shot
T/S = Top shot
M/CU = Medium close-up
C/U = Close-up
B/V = Back view
PAN = Shot in which camera is swung sideways from one object to another or following a moving object
TILT = Shot in which camera is swung vertically from one object to another or follows a moving object

Handicrafts

Not only is it far more fun and more satisfying to make things yourself, but it saves your pocket-money for the things which you *cannot* make. Here is the 'know-how' for some interesting 'make-it-yourself' projects, none of which needs special tools or equipment.

Making Model Railway Scenery

There's all the difference in the world between playing with toy trains and being a model railway enthusiast—and you can bridge that gap without digging deeply into your pocket. Scenery and buildings are expensive to buy; make them yourself at a fraction of the cost.

Scenery—hills, valleys, embankments, cliffs and so on—is best made from papier mâché. This doesn't involve fine modellers' papier mâché, which takes many hours to prepare. For tunnels, hills, etc., a rough, lumpy surface is realistic so lumpy papier mâché will do perfectly well. Fill a bucket with newspaper torn into small scraps, add a tablespoonful of size or a small square of carpenter's glue, then pour on boiling water and stir. Keep adding water and stirring until the mixture is like thick, lumpy porridge. let it cool enough to handle, and then use it to model your scenery. Painted in greens, brown and greys, it is far more realistic than any of the expensive scenery sold in modelling shops.

Railway buildings, houses, churches and factories are also easy to build, as long as you are satisfied with approximate scale. To reduce a building of your own local station to the standard '00' scale, count the number of bricks on an end wall, first vertically, then horizontally, and then allow seven bricks to the inch horizontally and twenty-two to the inch vertically.

Sturdy buildings can be made from card as long as the base is wooden. The method is very easy, and the sketch

216

below shows an example which is simple to adapt for other purposes. Once you understand how it's done, it requires only a little thought to apply it to any building of your own design.

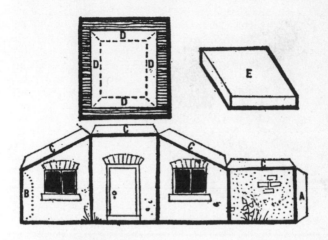

In this example of a plate-layer's hut, the roof could be painted grey or black and the walls covered with 'red-brick' paper—which costs only a few pence to buy. The chimney is a round wooden lollipop stick painted black. Before gluing A to B and C to D, fasten squares of cellophane on to the inside of each window. Finally, glue the completed building on to the base block E, which should fit snugly inside.

In this way stations, factories, houses and shops can be made cheaply and to designs which fit in with the layout of the track and the restrictions of space available.

217

Making Model Aircraft

Making scale model aircraft is a hobby which has grown rapidly in popularity in recent years due to the very large number of plastic kits now available at a price which many boys can afford. In these kits the parts come ready made and are well detailed. The modeller has to assemble the model and then paint and decorate it, often the part of the operation which is most fun. Tool kits can be built up as the modeller's ambitions increase. The most basic tools and materials are a craft knife, small file, glass paper, tweezers, dividers, steel rule, fine wire and fine paint brushes. Most of these items are usually found in the home already.

Models are made to various standard scales from very small 1 : 144 scale to a comparatively large 1 : 24 scale. Easily the most popular is the 1 : 72 scale. A collection will be most satisfying if all the models in it are to the same scale. When it comes to detailing, modellers need not follow the kitmaker's directions, but can make more individual models by converting into other aircraft. This may be no more complicated than merely changing the markings, to give a service aircraft, for instance, the decals and colours of a different Air Force from those supplied by the maker. Or it may be a more advanced conversion into another marque of the aircraft by amendments to cockpits or tailplanes. Conversion kits and decal sheets can be bought separately, but advanced modellers might like to make their own conversions with their own materials. A collection of reference material can be collected from aircraft books or magazines or from modelling magazines.

Rather than making models haphazardly, it is often wise to concentrate on a particular type of aircraft, for example British service planes of World War II. It will then be possible to make displays and dioramas of the finished models, and to make scenery for photographing the collection.

Many of the remarks made about making model aircraft apply to another fast-growing hobby, that of making model soldiers. Many military modelling or collecting societies have been formed in the last few years, and again the plastic kit, which allows considerable detail at a reasonable cost, has helped the boom.

Tools required are needle files, jeweller's engraving tools, jeweller's hand vice, razor saw, pliers, tweezers, craft knife, jeweller's metal scissors, nail scissors, steel rule, small drills, small C-clamps, paints and brushes. Tool sets are supplied by modelling manufacturers, but you will notice that some of the tools are used in the jewelery trade, and a jeweller's supplier will be able to provide good quality equipment at a reasonable price.

Beginners should start with plastic kits which are easier to work with, particularly if you want to animate your models. Much of the skill in making a good model comes with the painting. Paints may be matt enamel, acrylic or oil, or indeed a mixture of them, and are supplied by modelling shops.

Much of the fun in making a collection of model soldiers comes from the way you decide to present them. Small groups of figures can be arranged, or larger dioramas, even eventually whole battle scenes. Horses and mounted figures form a part of the model soldier scene. Bases for dioramas can be bought at modelling shops, but more satisfaction can be achieved at less cost by making your own from easily acquired materials like expanded polystyrene.

Bookbinding

Whole works have been written on the *proper* way to set about binding books at home, but the methods described require a heavy press. This simple way of putting sturdy covers on paper-backed books needs nothing except scraps of material, cardboard, scissors, glue and common sense.

First find a piece of stiff material big enough to cover the book with an inch to spare all round. If no stiff material is handy, use a piece of an old sheet, well starched. Cut out three pieces of cardboard, the sizes of the front, back and spine of the book. Glue these to the material as in the diagram.

Now cut slots at A, bend the material down and glue on to the card. Next glue B to the front and back of the book. Fold down and glue the edges of the material, being careful to make neat, flat folds at the corners. Finally, paste white paper on the inside of each cover, to hide the folds of the material. If you want the title of the book on the spine, neat lettering on a strip of white paper glued into place will finish off a thoroughly professional-looking job.

Printing from Linocuts

You can make black-and-white pictures or full-colour illustrations for Christmas cards and other purposes by linocut printing. A piece of high-quality thick lino is needed. This can be bought ready cut from an art materials shop in sizes from 3×3 inches upwards, or can be trimmed from scraps after laying household lino. Thin lino isn't suitable,

220

as the design for printing has to be cut into its surface. The lino should have a plain surface without any glossy design on it.

On the lino, draw the outlines of the picture which is to be made, remembering that the final result will be the exact reverse of your drawing. Avoid excessive detail; a picture drawn with a few bold strokes of the pencil is most likely to be successful. The outline should then be gone over with black India ink so that it will not be rubbed away by your hand while cutting the outlines.

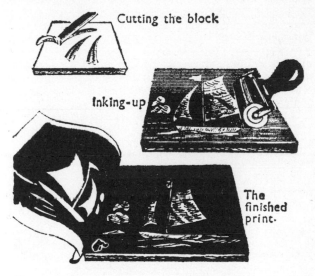

Cutting the block

Inking-up

The finished print.

You may already have a narrow 'V'-shaped chisel suitable for gouging out the unwanted areas of lino, but if not, one can be quite easily made from the broken rib of an old umbrella, fixed into a wooden handle and then ground to a sharp cutting edge. When all the areas which are not to be printed have been chiselled away, the picture is ready for inking.

This is done by means of a small roller and a piece of glass. The roller should be made of gelatine compound, and small ones can be obtained very cheaply at any art materials shop. So can small tubes of printing ink, and suitable paper.

Squeeze a small amount of printing ink on to the sheet of glass and work it to a thin, even surface with the roller which, of course, will then be similarly coated. Roll back and forth across the linocut; then place a sheet of printing paper on the linocut and press evenly and gently over the surface. This is best done with a circle of wood such as five-ply, of about four inches in diameter. This can easily be made with a fret-saw. The under side, which is to be used for pressing and rubbing, should have its edge smoothed off to prevent it from digging into the surface of the paper. Care should be taken that the lino does not slip while on the paper.

Linocuts in more than one colour can be made in the same way. A block is made for each colour of the full picture, and the only extra problem is that of making sure that all blocks 'register' accurately—in other words, that the colours do not overlap where this is not intended. If the picture is first drawn on to tracing paper and the appropriate outlines are then transferred on to each block of lino, this problem should not arise.

Making a Kite

Some designs of kite are hard to build, but this one takes only an hour or so and needs no complicated tools. Start with three straight sticks, one thirty inches long, the other with twenty-five inches in length. Nail the centres of the two shorter pieces to the centre of the long piece, and open out the shorter pieces so that, if the long piece pointed to twelve and six on the clock, the shorter pieces would be set at two, four, eight and ten. Make a small hole in the ends of each stick, and run a piece of very fine wire from hole to hole, securing it in each one with a knot. Then lay the framework on a piece of an old sheet, and cut out a section of sheet about one inch larger all round than the framework. Lap this extra inch round the wire so that the material is stretched fairly tightly and evenly over the framework, and sew it on.

Tie pieces of string about fifteen inches long to the four, six and eight o'clock struts; join the ends together and add a yard of extra string on which scraps of coloured paper have been knotted every few inches. Then, from the centre and from the ten, twelve, and two o'clock struts, run four more short lengths of string, joined at their ends. To this join is tied the end of the kite-string, which should be rolled on a stick when not in use.

Collecting as a Hobby

Stamp Collecting

Of all the hobbies there are, probably none has such widespread popularity as stamp collecting. Millions of people in the world today are, have been, or will be, stamp collectors.

The first postage stamps were issued in Britain, in 1840, to overcome the problem of standardising postal rates, which had become so high that most ordinary folk couldn't afford to send letters. The first country to follow Britain's lead was Brazil, in 1843, and by 1870 most of the principal nations had adopted the idea of stamps to pay postal charges. By that time the practice of collecting these stamps was firmly established. In those days, and indeed until twenty or thirty years ago, it was still possible to make a serious atempt to collect the stamps of all countries, but nowadays most 'philatelists' prefer to specialise. Here are a few suggestions for collections with plenty of scope yet which are reasonable enough in size to ensure that an active collector is not fighting a losing battle and collecting stamps more slowly than new ones are being issued:

Australasia
British Commonwealth Africa
British Commonwealth America
Great Britain, Cyprus, Gibraltar
    and Malta
British Commonwealth Asia
France and Colonies
Spain and Portugal, with their Colonies
North America
South America
The Caribbean
China and Japan

All of these are groups on which you can make a good start, by using parts of a general collection which has grown out of hand. But if you are really ambitious, you might like to choose 'thematics'—the modern idea of collecting stamps by subject rather than by countries. This way you can make a collection which will serve as an aid to your other interests and hobbies. The following are subjects on which enough stamps have been issued to make any one of them suitable for a large collection:

    The history of aviation
    The sea and shipping
    World transport
    Engineering
    Botany
    Birds, animals and fishes
    World sport
    Exploration
    Scouting, and other youth movements

But in making a choice what could be better than inventing your own theme—an original one which you can feel sure will make yours the only collection of its kind?

Collecting Match-box Labels

Collecting match-box labels, like stamp collecting, is a hobby dating back to the last century. You set about it by saving all you can find and making exchanges with other collectors for the ones you need.

Remove the labels from the boxes by soaking them for a few minutes in hot water, peeling them off, and then drying them between sheets of blotting paper. Loose-leaf albums are the best for mounting collections, and stamp-hinges will safely fix them to the page.

British match-box labels are usually rather dull and uninteresting in design, but there are thousands of foreign ones with highly-coloured action pictures on them. You can find labels showing portraits of native warriors, ships and planes, railways, and you can find some with exciting forgeries printed by wartime resistance groups, bearing slogans encouraging the guerrilla fighters.

Coin Collecting

This is a hobby in which the lucky collector can still come across rare finds of great value or tremendous historical interest. Unlike stamps and match-box labels, coins can be lost for centuries and still survive undamaged, and it is not unusual, when new ground is being turned over or old buildings are being demolished, for coins dating back even as far as Roman times to be unearthed. Coins have been in existence since about 700 B.C., and appeared in Britain before the last century B.C.

Modern coins of many countries can be obtained easily through exchange or by buying a bag of assorted foreign coins.

A cabinet to house your collection needs shallow drawers lined with baize into which holes have been cut to let the coins lie snugly without moving. A small gummed identification label can be stuck below each coin.

Cigarette-card Collecting

Cigarette manufacturers no longer issue cards in their packets, but for many years, until 1939, there was a card in nearly every packet in Britain, the Commonwealth and many other countries. Millions of these have survived, and so it is still possible to start collecting. But the wise collector will look beyond cigarette cards to include *all* cards of a similar kind—which means the many issued in packets and boxes of tea and sweets. Sets, usually of twenty-five or fifty, range in subject from great sportsmen to ocean fishes, from ancient weapons to Derby winners. Many cards issued in the ten years before World War II were accompanied by albums for mounting them.

Older relatives may be able to add to your collection, and cards may also be purchased from dealers.

Cheese-label Collecting

The proper name for this is 'fromology', and the makers of cheese in many countries have recognised the rapid growth of the hobby in recent years by issuing many new and colourful designs. It is possible to build up a collection of more than thirty thousand different labels by exchanging with other collectors. The original source of supply is, of course, your own family kitchen. Friends travelling abroad and pen pals in foreign countries can help to enlarge your collection.

A collection of cheese labels is best mounted and stored in the same way as a stamp collection, using stamp-hinges to fasten the labels in place in a safe way so that they can be removed for exchange or remounting without damage. Removing labels which are gummed tightly to the wrapping of the cheese is best done without using water, as certain labels have colours which 'run' when moistened. Suitable methods are levering the label off the paper by cautious work with a paper knife or peeling off one corner and allowing steam from a kettle to penetrate the glue without coming into direct contact with the printed surface.

There are plenty of different pictorial subjects on cheese labels, ranging from wild animals, flowers and country scenes to aircraft, ships and sportsmen.

This is a hobby for those who enjoy reading and who are, perhaps, interested in writing as well. And though buying new books is expensive, collecting old ones is a hobby that, if carried out carefully, need cost no more than a few pence a week.

Your own interests and other hobbies will help you to decide the subjects which will form the basis of your collection. There are, of course, hundreds to choose from, but a few which can make absorbingly interesting collections without much cost are:

Printing—its history and development
Your favourite sport
What towns and countries looked like in the past
Early cars and railways
Wild life at home and abroad

These suggestions have been made bearing in mind the available sources of old books—second-hand book shops, junk shops and auction rooms. Very often at small auctions you can buy odd lots of books fifty or a hundred years old for prices as low as fifty pence for a hundred. Of this hundred, ninety-five are likely to be completely useless to you, but exchanges with other collectors, or even subsequent auctions, will enable you to get rid of the ones you don't want.

Condition is important if you are collecting books for their own sake, but if you are simply hoping, for instance, to accumulate pictures and information about early railways, you will not be unduly worried if some of your books have torn covers and missing pages. Damaged books can be repaired quite easily (see *Bookbinding,* page 219) so your bookcases need not remain untidy simply because your books, when you bought them, were in shabby condition.

Collecting Pottery

Collectors of rare china pay thousands of pounds for individual pieces of particular quality and historical interest, but you can have just as much fun for a few pence and build up a collection with as much variety. Auction rooms and junk shops have large quantities of old china and pottery which change hands for very low prices, and though much of it is rubbish, now and again rare and attractive oddments can be found among the heaps of old teacups and pie-dishes. But if this doesn't appeal to you then the collecting of modern pottery may. In Britain, and in many other countries, there are small 'one-man' potteries producing excellent craftsmanship. If you buy their work at fashionable shops you will have to pay high prices for it, but if on holiday in Devon and Cornwall for example, you visit some of these tiny potteries, you can buy the same articles for a considerably lower price.

Keeping Pets

Dogs

Choosing a dog for a pet needs careful thought. It isn't enough to decide, 'That's for me!' when a friendly puppy in a pet shop rolls his eyes at you and licks your hand. What you have to consider is the size he will reach, the amount of exercise he'll need, and the amount he is likely to eat. You also have to make up your mind whether the desire to have a dog is just a passing fancy or a feeling that will remain, for when you have bought or been given a dog not only does that dog belong to you, *but you belong to him*. Dogs have as intense a feeling of loyalty as do human beings, and an unwanted dog feels just as lost as an unwanted person does.

There are many breeds from which to choose a dog that suits your requirements; or you may prefer a mongrel to a pedigree pup. Your local dogs' home will be able to help you there. Remember that a large dog can be an encumbrance in a flat or a small house—and his food bills will be high. A dog bred for an active open-air life may be unhappy in a town. So think it over carefully before making your choice.

As soon as you get your dog, buy him a licence if he is over six months old. This can be obtained at any Post Office. It is against the law to keep a dog without a licence.

He will need a box or basket. Dog baskets are rather expensive, but a comfortable box can be made out of scrap wood without any difficult carpentry. Make it big enough for him to move about in and to stretch in his sleep, yet cosy enough to keep him warm. The box should be in a corner free from draughts, and should be lined with several newspapers to keep in the warmth. On top of these he should have an old rug or blanket, or, alternatively, an old eiderdown. Don't just give him a pillow; most dogs like to roll themselves up in their bedding, just as many of us do. The bedding should be taken out of doors and shaken every day or two and the newspaper changed at frequent intervals.

If you have a garden and your dog is able to get plenty of exercise in it, then one short walk every day should be all he needs. Except in country districts, this should preferably be on a lead.

He will probably be untrained when you first get him. Training needs patience, and if it seems to take a long time, remember that the training of a human baby takes far longer. It will help your puppy if you can start off with a regular routine of meals, walks and grooming.

At first, puppies need to be let out of doors every two or three hours during the day. A few messes indoors must be expected, and the dog which learns quickly is the one which is praised for attending to his needs out of doors rather than the one which is punished for making a mess in the hall.

Teach your dog to 'come to heel' when taken out of doors without a lead. A little perseverance should make him completely obedient to your orders. A disobedient dog is less to blame than his owner, for a dog naturally regards man as his master and disobeys only when that master no longer deserves respect. To earn that respect, you have to be absolutely consistent about discipline. If your dog is punished or spoken to sharply for making a mess on the pavements then he must *always* be punished or spoken to sharply for it. If he is praised when he comes to heel promptly, then he must *always* be praised. Above all, he must never be punished without knowing why.

Grooming needs vary for different breeds of dogs. Short-haired dogs need only a brisk rub-down from time to time with a rough towel or a brush; long-haired varieties need more frequent attention, with a steel comb and stiff brush. Your dog should be taught to look forward to this as a regular habit and should be complimented on his smartness afterwards. Washing need not be frequent for most breeds and should be done either with ordinary toilet soap or with dog soap sold by your pet-shop. Don't use kitchen soap, as the soda will harm his coat as well as irritate the pores of his skin. The temperature of the water should be moderate. Immediately after his bath your dog should be very thoroughly dried, otherwise he'll undertake this himself and in doing so probably make himself dirtier than he was before.

A dog's diet should consist of about a half ounce of meat for each pound of his weight, as well as about the same amount of cereal and vegetable matter. The quantities required must be adjusted according to the amount of exercise the dog gets. It is as important not to over-feed as it is not to under-feed, as over-feeding brings about various stomach troubles which may be difficult to cure.

Meat should not be overcooked, and many dogs prefer it raw. Bones, carefully chosen in order to avoid those which may cause injury through sharp splinters, are used by most dogs more as playthings than as a source of food, and to compensate a dog for the lack of mineral from bones he should be given a small amount of ground bone-meal in his diet.

A puppy should be fed four or five times a day, but by the time a dog is fully grown he should be fed only one main meal a day and should know the exact time at which to expect his food. Your dog should always have access to a supply of fresh water.

Cats

A kitten is ready to leave its mother at eight weeks, by which time it should have learned to attend to its needs out of doors or in an ash-box placed in a corner. A cat needs the same kind of bedding as a dog, also the same chance to go out of doors for exercise. Do not attempt to

232

help a cat keep itself clean; unlike dogs, cats spend much of their time doing this very efficiently, and your assistance will not be appreciated.

Kittens should receive several feeds a day, but by the time they are six months old this should have been reduced to two, or even one, given at regular times of the day. A healthy adult cat should receive about half an ounce of food for every pound it weighs. Milk, meat, fish, liver, and most table scraps, providing they do not contain too much spice, are their basic diet. A cat should always have access to a supply of fresh water.

Mice

All varieties of tame mice need a warm temperature, and must be given a cage with plenty of room. Its floor should be littered with clean sawdust, which should be changed frequently. Grain mixture and bread is the ideal diet, with fragments of cheese and greenstuff. The water supply must be kept fresh.

Hamsters

Golden hamsters are kept in the same way as mice. As well as bread and cereal, they enjoy carrots, maize meal and milk.

Guinea-pigs

Guinea-pigs are best kept out of doors in a warm shed which is thoroughly proofed against rats, cats and dogs. They should have an outdoor run on the sheltered side of their shed. The shed itself should contain plenty of litter for bedding; wood-wool or fine shavings are ideally suitable for this. The bedding should be changed frequently to avoid unpleasant smells and the danger of disease. Guinea-pigs need about an ounce of cereal daily (bran and crushed oats), with a plentiful supply of garden greenstuff. Fresh water should always be available.

Rabbits

Rabbits require much the same housing as guinea-pigs but the food may be more varied. Rabbits will thrive on many kinds of household scraps, such as bread, cooked potatoes and plenty of green food.

Tortoises

A tortoise, as he carries his own house with him, needs only a shelter to keep off heavy rain and wind. A small wooden box on its side in the garden is adequate. In a garden which contains plants of value it may be necessary to limit the tortoise's movements by boards or low fencing, for he will spend much of his time wandering about and sampling different kinds of greenstuff. In winter he will hibernate, and it is important to know *where*, as once this has happened he must not be disturbed until the warmer weather returns. If brought into a greenhouse or shed to hibernate in a box, he should be given plenty of straw and dry leaves with which to cover himself completely. If he hibernates in the garden, he will probably fail to cover himself with a thick enough layer of earth to keep out the frost, and so a thick wad of straw should be placed on top.

During the summer the moisture from greenstuff may be insufficient; a tortoise should then be given a supply of fresh water in a shallow plate or saucer.

Cage Birds

Canaries require a diet composed of canary seed, summer rape seed, cuttlefish bone and a little greenstuff. Fresh water should always be provided in the cage. Budgerigars should receive millet and canary seed, with lettuce or other greenstuff in small quantities. The secret of successful bird-keeping is attention to cleanliness; the cage must be kept spotlessly clean and the waterchanged as often as possible. Care must also be taken to prevent draughts.

Easy-to-Grow Flowers

If starting a small corner of your own in the family garden, prepare the ground by digging over thoroughly and removing weeds and grass. Work in any compost or old manure before planting. Here are some flowers which are easy to grow, some of which you might like to try in your own garden. (Remember, annuals are plants which last only a single year; biennials flower in their second year and then die; perennials live on from year to year.)

Ageratum is a half-hardy annual, with mauve, pink, blue or white flowers, 6 to 9 inches (150—230 mm) in height. It is sown under glass in early spring.

Alyssum is a useful hardy annual for sunny borders and rockeries. It can be sown in the open and has mauve or white flowers. Perennial varieties are also available. Height 3 to 6 inches (75—150 mm).

Antirrhinum, usually known as *Snapdragon,* can be grown as an annual or kept as a perennial. It is sown under glass from January to March and planted out in May. Height ranges from 6 inches to 3 feet (150—900 mm); all colours are available except blue.

Armeria, also called *Thrift,* is a cushiony, hardy perennial with red, pink or white flowers, ideal for borders and rockeries. Height 6 inches (150 mm).

Aster, a family of half-hardy annuals available in many colours, includes the *Michaelmas Daisy*—a hardy perennial which ranges from blue and mauve to pale pink and white.

China Aster, sown in May, are ideal as cut flowers.

Aubrietia is a trailing rock plant (hardy perennial) with

235

purple or pink flowers. It is best grown from cuttings.

Calendula, or *Pot Marigold,* a half-hardy annual with double or single flowers, ranges from pale yellow to a rich gold. Sown in early spring, it should provide plenty of colour in late summer. Height 18 to 30 inches (450—750 mm).

Candytuft is grown from seed as a hardy annual or perennial. The average height is 12 inches (300 mm); the spiked flowers are pink, crimson or lilac.

Cheiranthus, or *Siberian Wallflower,* is available in yellow and orange. Sown in May and transplanted after reaching a height of 2 inches (50 mm), it flowers the following year. Height 18 inches (450 mm).

Chrysanthemums are of two kinds. The hardy annuals are sown in the open in spring for summer flowering; the perennials can be grown from cuttings and root division. There are many varieties and shades, and chrysanthemums are the mainstay of the autumn flower-bed. Height 18 inches to 3 feet (450—900 mm).

Clarkia is hardy annual with pastel or white flowers. It is sown in April and grows to about 24 inches (600 mm) in height.

Cornflower, a hardy annual, is easy to grow and has a wide range of colours. Height 2 to 2½ feet (600—750 mm).

Crocus is a hardy perennial, yellow, white or purple, with a corm or bulb which is planted in the early autumn for flowering the following spring.

Dahlia is a half-hardy perennial with a tuberous root. It can be raised from seed, and after flowering the tubers can be stored away from frost for replanting the next year. It comes in a variety of colours, and varies in size from 18 inches to 5 feet (450—1,500 mm).

Delphinium is of two varieties. The annual, known as *Larkspur,* is planted as seed in the spring; the perennial is often raised from cuttings planted in spring or autumn. It is usually available in various shades of blue and is from 2 to 6 feet (600—1,800 mm) in height.

Dianthus is the family which includes the *Carnation, Pink* and *Sweet William*. Hardy border carnations are propagated by cutting, and so are pinks. Sweet Williams are grown from seed as biennials.

Gladiolus is a tall flowering plant grown from a corm planted in the spring. In early autumn the corms are lifted and the new offset corms removed and stored to start fresh plants the next spring. The plant grows from 30 inches to 4½ feet (750—1,350 mm) in height and is available in a wide variety of colours.

Gypsophila is a pink or white annual, grown from seed in March. A perennial variety can be raised from root division. Height about 18 inches (450 mm).

Hyacinth is a bulb planted in October for spring flowering, or in pots indoors from August onwards for mid-winter. Available in many colours, it grows to about 12 inches (300 mm) in height.

Iris is a hardy perennial with roots that divide easily for propagation in the late autumn. It is available in a great variety of heights and colours.

Lobelia is best started under glass in early spring. The mass of blue or white flowers it produces is ideal for borders and rockeries.

Love-in-a-Mist is an annual with blue or white flowers, and is sown in the open in March or April. Height 18 inches (450 mm).

Narcissus is a class of bulb which includes the *Daffodil*. It is planted in the late summer or early autumn for spring flowering, and need not be lifted except when so many new bulbs have formed that splitting becomes necessary.

Nasturtium is sown in the open as soon as the danger of frost is past. There are many varieties, ranging from pale yelow to deep orange in colour.

Phlox is a hardy annual or perennial available in a variety of colours. The annual is sown under glass in spring for summer flowering; the perennial is best increased by cuttings in early spring or October. Height from 1 to 5 feet (300—1,500 mm).

Primula is a member of the family which includes *Primroses* and *Polyanthus*. All varieties can be raised from seed, but the usual method is by splitting old plants after flowering has ended.

Roses are best planted in early November. There are a number of types, such as ramblers, bushes and standards, climbers and polyanthus. Most varieties need pruning for good results. In general, the rule is that strong growers are lighty pruned and weak growers need more severe treatment.

Sweet Pea is a hardy annual grown mainly for cut flowers. Sown in autumn or spring, it requires good, well-manured soil. The more sweet peas are picked, the more they flower. The range of colours and sizes is considerable.

Tulip is a hardy perennial bulb plant for early spring flowering. It is planted in autumn in the open. It can also be grown indoors in pots.

Garden Calendar

January. Take cuttings of chrysanthemums from the bases of old plants and set them in pots containing leaf-mould and old mortar. Sow sweet peas in boxes under glass.

February. Plant onions, leeks, shallots and early peas in the open. Sow spinach, parsnips and early carrots if the ground is not frozen.

March. Plant broccoli, Brussels sprouts, cabbage, carrots, cauliflower, lettuce, peas, potatoes, parsley, radishes and summer cabbages in the open. Plant pinks and carnations, and begin sowing annuals.

April. Plant French beans, cauliflower, beetroot, celery, lettuce, mustard and cress, peas, potatoes, spinach, summer turnips and marrows. Sow remaining annuals, and plant shrubs.

May. Plant further crops of potatoes, lettuce and cabbage.

238

Sow runner beans, further annuals, also sweet williams, wallflowers, forget-me-nots and Canterbury bells. Plant early chrysanthemums.

June. Plant tomatoes, sweet corn and cucumber. Plant dahlia tubers and hardy perennials.

July. Plant out winter cabbages. Sow further annuals for autumn flowering, and plant out biennials sown in May.

August. Sow winter spinach, winter swedes and turnips in the open. Plant crocuses, narcissi and snowdrops, as well as bulbs in fibre for indoor display.

September. Continue sowing winter vegetables. Harvest root crops and gather tomatoes. Plant irises and additional narcissi and crocuses.

October. Plant spring cabbages. Lift dahlias and gladioli. Prepare soil for roses.

November. Sow broad beans. Plant and transplant trees and shrubs. Plant cuttings from perennials and also increase them by root-splitting. Plant roses.

December. Start of the best season for digging. Remove weeds. Prepare trenches for sweet peas. Take chrysanthemum cuttings.

Judging the Weather

The following is a rough guide to judging the weather by means of a household barometer.

1. If the needle or mercury is rising, calm or fair weather can be expected.
2. If the needle or mercury is falling, expect rain and unsettled weather.
3. A rising and falling barometer indicates changeable weather.
4. A steady barometer means that the weather is likely to continue as at the time of reading.
5. A very slow rise or fall indicates the approach of a good or bad settled condition.

Indoor Games

Indoor games can be excellent fun, especially as your skill in mastering them increases. Here are the rules of a few of the standard games:

Chess

The game is for two players, one taking the white players and the other the black. The board is of sixty-four squares, alternately black and white. At the beginning of the game each player has a white square in the right-hand corner nearest him. The lines of squares going from left to right are called *ranks,* those from top to bottom *files,* and the paths from corner to corner and those parallel to them are called *diagonals.*

Each player has sixteen pieces: a king (K), a queen (Q), two rooks (R) (or castles), two bishops (B), two knights (Kt) and eight pawns (P). At the beginning of the game the pieces are laid out as in the diagram. Note that the white queen occupies a white square, and the black queen opposite occupies a black square. White moves first. When games of chess are described each square has a number, or rather two, one with reference to the white pieces, and one to the black. These are shown in the second diagram. If in the first move of the game the pawn on the square QB2 (known as the queen's bishop pawn) is moved two squares forward the move will be written thus: 1. QBP — QB4.

The object of the game is to capture the opponent's king. Pieces capture an enemy piece by moving to the square occupied by that piece, the captured piece being removed from the board.

Pieces move as follows:

King: one square in any direction, either along a rank, a file or diagonally.

Queen :   any number of squares in any direction.

Rook :   any number of squares along a rank or file.

Bishop :   any number of squares diagonally. It follows that a bishop on a white square can only move to another white square.

Knight :   two squares along a rank or file and then one square to left or right. If you look at the diagram, the knight on QKt1 can make his first move to QR3, QB3 or Q2. A knight in the centre of the board will have eight possible squares to move to. A knight is the only piece on the board that may jump over other pieces.

Pawn :   A pawn on his first move may move either one or two squares along his file. Subsequently he may

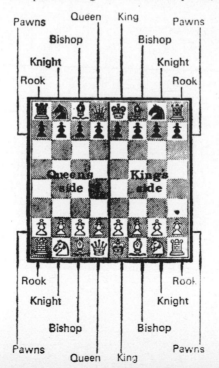

241

move only one square forward. Pawns, unlike other pieces may only move forwards towards the opponent's end of the board. If a pawn reaches the end of its file, it may be exchanged for another piece, usually, of course, the most powerful, the Queen. A player by this means may have two queens on the board. When capturing an opponent's piece, however, a pawn moves one square forward diagonally, either to left or right.

BLACK

QR1 / QR8	QKt1 / QKt8	QB1 / QB8	Q1 / Q8	K1 / K8	KB1 / KB8	KKt1 / KKt8	KR1 / KR8
QR2 / QR7	QKt2 / QKt7	QB2 / QB7	Q2 / Q7	K2 / K7	KB2 / KB7	KKt2 / KKt7	KR2 / KR7
QR3 / QR6	QKt3 / QKt6	QB3 / QB6	Q3 / Q6	K3 / K6	KB3 / KB6	KKt3 / KKt6	KR3 / KR6
QR4 / QR5	QKt4 / QKt5	QB4 / QB5	Q4 / Q5	K4 / K5	KB4 / KB5	KKt4 / KKt5	KR4 / KR5
QR5 / QR4	QKt5 / QKt4	QB5 / QB4	Q5 / Q4	K5 / K4	KB5 / KB4	KKt5 / KKt4	KR5 / KR4
QR6 / QR3	QKt6 / QKt3	QB6 / QB3	Q6 / Q3	K6 / K3	KB6 / KB3	KKt6 / KKt3	KR6 / KR3
QR7 / QR2	QKt7 / QKt2	QB7 / QB2	Q7 / Q2	K7 / K2	KB7 / KB2	KKt7 / KKt2	KR7 / KR2
QR8 / QR1	QKt8 / QKt1	QB8 / QB1	Q8 / Q1	K8 / K1	KB8 / KB1	KKt8 / KKt1	KR8 / KR1

WHITE

There are two other special moves. The first is the *en passant* move. As stated, a pawn may move on its first move two squares forward, but if by doing so it avoids capture by an opposing pawn (i.e. if by moving only one square forward an opposing pawn could have taken it), then the opposing player may capture the pawn *en passant,* and may take it as if it had moved only one square.

The second special move is known as "castling". If a player has not moved his king or the rook on his king's side, but the intervening squares are empty, he may castle by moving his king to KKt1 and his rook to KB1. This is known as castling on the king's side. Similarly, he may castle on the queen's side by moving his king to QB1 and his rook to Q1. A player may not castle if his king is in check (which will be explained later), nor may he castle more than once in a game.

How does a player win by capturing his opponent's king? First, the expression "check" must be explained. If a player has one or more of his pieces so positioned that he may capture his opponent's king on the next move, then that king is in check, and the attacking-player must announce "check". The opponent must then use his next move to avert the danger, which can be done by capturing the threatening piece, by moving one of his own pieces to an interposing square to block the threat, or by moving his king to a safe square. If none of these alternatives is open to him, then the king is "checkmated", and the game is lost.

A game can be drawn at any time by agreement. A game is also drawn if stalemate occurs, which is when a player can move only his king, which is not in check, but can move it only to a position of check. A draw by repetition can be claimed if a position repeats itself three times, or if a player can place his opponent's king in perpetual check: that is, if a player cannot checkmate but can check the opposing king on every move, he may claim a draw.

At the beginning of a game, a player should attempt to get

his more powerful pieces into play as quickly as possible. For example, if the pawn in front of the king is moved, diagonals are immediately opened up for the queen and a bishop. There are several recognized openings to chess games, each with a name, and there are recognized counters to them, all designed to achieve good positions early in the game. There are many books published on opening gambits, as they are called, as indeed there are on all stages of a chess game, and a beginner who wishes to play well should obtain and study one of the books designed for learners.

Draughts

This is played on the black squares of a chess-board, using two sets of men, each consisting of twelve black and twelve red or white circular pieces. These are arranged on the black squares of the first three rows at each end of the board, and move one square forward, diagonally. The purpose of the game is to capture all the opponent's pieces, which is done by jumping across them to a vacant square beyond. If, by so doing, the attacker then lands on a square from which it is able to capture again, it does so without waiting for the next move. On reaching the opponent's back line, a piece becomes a King by having a captured piece placed on top, and thenceforward may move forward or back.

A player in a position to make a capture must do so.

Backgammon

This game has had a great revival of interest in the 1970s. It is for two players. It is played with a special board, fifteen black and fifteen white counters or stones and two dice. The illustration shows the board set out at the beginning of the game. The board is divided by a bar into two halves; by arrangement one half is the inner table and one half the outer—in the illustration the left half is the inner. Projecting from each side of the board are twelve points of alternate colours (numbered in the illustration for convenience, but not numbered on the board itself). Each player rolls one die, and the higher plays first. The object is to move all fifteen stones into the inner table and thence off the board. The first player to bear off his stones is the winner. Each player moves towards his inner table (i.e. white moves clockwise in the illustration, black anti-clockwise).

The first player rolls both dice and may move his stones according to his score. He may move two stones, each according to the score of one die, or he may move the same stone twice. For instance, if White rolls 6—3, he may move one stone from Black's point 1 to point 10, or he may move one stone from Black 12 to White 7 and one from Black 12 to

INNER TABLE BLACK OUTER TABLE

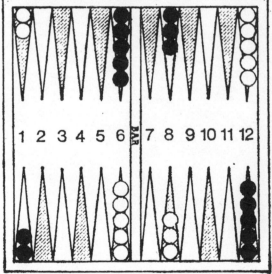

INNER TABLE WHITE OUTER TABLE

White 10. Doubles are scored twice over, for instance a double-6 would enable the player to move four stones each six points, or, if he prefers, two stones twelve points. A player must always move if possible. If he cannot move, he loses the turn. If he can move only the score on one die, he must, and if he can move the score on either die, but not both, he must take the higher score.

No point may be occupied by stones of opposite colours. If a player has two or more stones on a point, he has made the point, and the other player must not land on it. Thus if Whites first throw is 5-5, he cannot move either stone on Black's point 1, as the first 5 would take either to Black's point 6, which is already occupied by five Black stones. A single stone on a point is called a blot. If the opponent can move a stone to that point, the blot is hit and is removed from the board and placed on the bar in the centre of the board. When a player's stone is on the bar, he must enter it before he moves any other stone. A stone enters on the adverse inner table. Thus if Black has a stone on the bar, and White has two stones on each point of his own inner table, it is clear that Black cannot move, and must wait until a point is available before he can enter his stone.

A player's first task is to move all fifteen stones into his inner table. Once he has achieved this, he may begin to bear off his stones. A stone is borne off by throwing the number equivalent to the point occupied by the stone. Thus if White has all his stones in his inner table, and throws 4-2, he may bear off stones from points 4 and 2. Or, of course, he may bear off one stone from point, 6. Or, if he wishes, he may bear off a stone from point 2, and move a stone from point 6 to point 2. If, at this stage of the game, a player throws a number higher than his highest occupied point, he may bear off a stone from his highest occupied point. For example, if he throws a 6, and his highest occupied point is 5, he may bear off the stone on point 5.

It will be seen that backgammon is in effect a race, with

each player moving his stones in opposite directions round the board in an attempt to bear them all off first. A player should try to make points, which render his own stones safe for the time being and also impede his opponent's stones. It is impossible to avoid blots altogether, but it should be noted that if a blot is hit and placed on the bar it is easier to enter it early in the game than it might be later when an opponent may have made some of his inner table points.

Secret Codes

The simplest secret codes are made by merely advancing every letter of every word by two, three or four in the alphabet; thus, using a four-stage code, the word 'alphabet' would become 'eptlefix'. Rapid coding and decoding of messages using this system can be done by drawing a large circle and writing the alphabet round it, leaving equal distances between each letter. A smaller circle is cut out of a sheet of paper, and the alphabet written once more round it. This is pinned to the centre of the larger circle, so that it can be rotated. Move it four stages forward, and every letter is moved by the same amount.

But this kind of code can be solved very easily, and for messages of top secrecy a more complicated code can be made with very little trouble. Both the sender and receiver of the code message must agree in advance upon a secret code word. It can be any word as long as no letter occurs more than once. Let's say, for example, that it is the word 'DIVER'.

Draw a square and divide it into twenty-five small squares. Starting at the top left-hand corner, fill in the letters of the code word, one in each square, and then the remaining letters of the alphabet in correct order, omitting the ones used already and also omitting 'J', because as we have only twenty-five squares the same code symbol has to serve for both 'I' and 'J'.

The method of coding and decoding may at first seem rather complicated, but a little practise will enable you to carry it out rapidly. Begin by dividing your message into pairs of letters. Thus 'DO NOT RETURN TO BASE would become 'DO NO TR ET UR NT OB AS EQ'. The letter 'Q' is added as a dummy to complete the final pair.

Now your code square, with 'DIVER' as its code word, looks like this:

D	I	V	E	R
A	B	C	F	G
H	K	L	M	N
O	P	Q	S	T
U	W	X	Y	Z

Looking at your pairs of letters waiting for coding, you can see that any two letters are either on the same vertical line, such as 'DO', on the same horizontal line, or at opposite corners of a square or rectangle. If the letters are in the same vertical column, each is translated into code by using the next letter above it, the very top letter of a column being coded by the one at the bottom. Thus 'DO' becomes 'UH' in code. A group on the same horizontal line is coded by using for each letter the one immediately on its right, with the end right-hand letter coded by the one at the extreme left. Letters at opposite corners of a square or rectangle are coded by taking the letters at the other corners of the square or rectangle, so that 'NO' becomes 'HT', and 'ET' becomes 'RS'. The original message, 'DO NOT RETURN TO BASE', becomes, in code, 'UH HT NZ RS ZD GN PA FO VS'. To decode this when receiving at the other end, you simply work the whole process in reverse, using a similar code square. The only other factor to be remembered is that it is impossible to code a pair of identical letters, such as 'BB' or 'OO', for obvious reasons, and it is necessary, therefore, to put a 'Q' between them while dividing the message into groups.

There are many other codes in use, but though some of them are very much more complicated, nearly all of them depend upon the principle used in this twenty-five-square system.

Personal Record

The following section is about *you*. We've dealt with facts and figures on hundreds of subjects of world-wide importance; now what about yourself? Where do *you* fit in, and what kind of person are you? Here, then, is the personal record which not only reminds you of facts and figures which may otherwise get lost or forgotten but helps you to find out more about yourself.

Full Name:
Date of Birth:
Address:
Telephone Number:
School: *School Number:*
Savings Book Number:
Club Number:
Medical Card Number:
Position in School:

Term	Year	Class	Position
Spring	19		
Summer	19		
Autumn	19		
Spring	19		
Summer	19		
Autumn	19		
Spring	19		
Summer	19		
Autumn	19		

Weight and Height Charts

These two graphs will help you to note your own progress. As you fill in the dots marking your height and weight at different ages, link them up to form a line from the bottom left corner to the top right of each graph.

Height

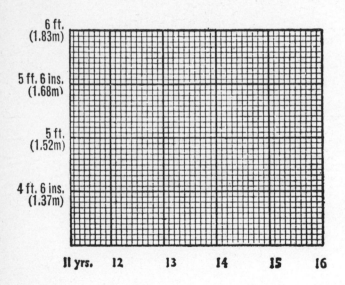

Height

Weight

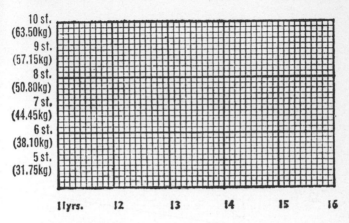

11yrs.	12	13	14	15	16

Athletics Charts

If you want to check your athletics performances against a standard, the following rough set of standards is suggested as average for boys of certain ages. However, if you are just twelve years old, do not be depressed if your standard is below that suggested for 12—13 year olds, as your performance could improve considerably in a few months.

Average Performances for Boys

Event	Age 12—13	Age 13—14	Age 14—15	Age 15—16
100 metres	13.1 s.	12.8 s.	12.5 s.	11.6 s.
100 yards	11.9 s.	11.6 s.	11.4 s.	10.5 s.
200 metres	30.3 s.	29.8 s.	28.8 s.	27.3 s.
220 yards	30.5 s.	30 s.	29 s.	27.5 s.
400 metres	---	69.5 s.	67 s.	63.5 s.

251

440 yards	—	70 s.	67.5 s.	64 s.
800 metres	—	2 min. 44 s.	2 min. 30 s.	2 min. 26 s.
880 yards	—	2 min. 45 s.	2 min. 31 s.	2 min. 27 s.
Long jump	—	4.27 m.	4.55 m.	4.67 m.
High jump	—	1.24 m.	1.34 m.	1.41 m.
Discus	—	21.33 m.	27.50 m.	30.00 m.
Javelin	—	21 m. 33 m.	29.00 m.	32.00 m.
Shot putt	—	6.00 m.	9.00 m.	10.67 m.

Charts such as the following show you how to keep records of your own best performances each season, and lines drawn to join each entry to the next will reveal how steady your improvement is.

Shot Putt

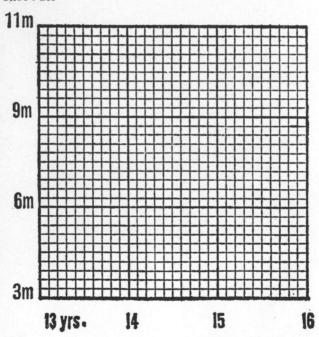

Long Jump

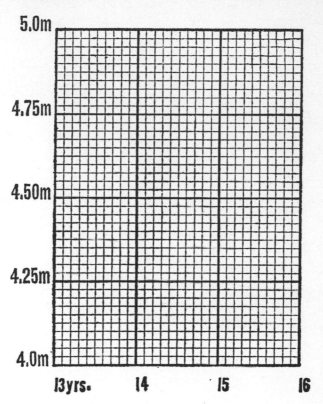

5.0m			
4.75m			
4.50m			
4.25m			
4.0m			

13yrs.   14   15   16

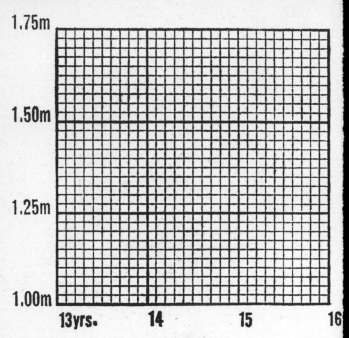